Why Don't We Learn from History ?

Why Don't We Learn from History?

B. H. Liddell Hart

Edited, & with an Introduction by Giles Laurén

SOPHRON 2112

ISBN 978 0985081133
098 50811 39

Sir Basil Henry Liddell Hart (1895-1970)

Design by Sophron

PREFACE

At the time of his death in 1970 my father had been preparing a revised and expanded edition of a short book of historical reflections which he had published in 1944. During the last twenty-five years of his life and until the end, he had continued to be both prolific in the writing of history and influential in the making of it. Besides numerous articles on current international and military affairs, he wrote, edited, or prefaced a number of works on subjects that had by then become part of history. He published his own memoirs in 1965-1966, covering in two volumes his career up to the outbreak of World War II. Finally he completed his history of that war and was, in fact, correcting the proofs of this long-awaited work at the time of his death.

He was, too, the unofficial adviser to an ever-widening circle of political and military leaders throughout the world. He had a vast correspondence. He traveled incessantly, often at the invitation of foreign governments and services, as a lecturer and consultant. In his seventieth year he went to be Visiting Professor of Military History at the University of California. To his country house in England came a constant flow of visitors seeking his advice and assistance and availing themselves of the facilities for research which with the support of London University he had built up in his unique library there.

To a whole generation of new historians he became a mentor, just as many of their contemporaries in the services of many countries, now often in high command, regarded themselves as his disciples. Having himself become prominent at a remarkably early age, at the end of World War I, he was personally linked with events and figures which had already passed into history: the friend as well as the biographer of Lawrence of Arabia, the collaborator of Lloyd George in his own memoirs of World War I and in ensuing controversies, the ally as well as the critic of Winston Churchill during the interwar years.

Over half a century of public life problems and personalities changed, but in his approach to them, as to life, he never grew old.

It is against this background and in this personal perspective that his contribution to history, and his reflections on it, should be rightly assessed. Immensely thorough, he was not an academic historian as the term is usually understood. His first degree was an honorary doctorate from Oxford University. Although he had studied and published books on remoter periods, from the Roman wars to the American Civil War, he was predominantly concerned with events which could be checked through firsthand sources. He was a meticulous recorder of such events in his own notes of discussions. Wherever possible he visited the scenes of the campaigns which he was to describe or revisited them; he had fought on the Western Front himself. He was a professional journalist, even a popular journalist, who continued to use the press not only as a means of influence and communication but as filed material for historical study. Moreover he remained actively interested in many aspects of history, from religion to fashion, which were outside the specialised military sphere with which his reputation was identified.

He was a historian who strove for rigorous objectivity and maintained intellectual detachment throughout the crises of his life and despite the official, commercial or personal pressures to which he was inevitably exposed. He valued and to a remarkable extent succeeded in preserving his independence of inquiry, judgment and expression, even in time of war. He was, too, a resolute defender of other people's rights in this respect and under different regimes. He was not indifferent or neutral. On many contemporary and even historical issues he felt strongly, even passionately. He would always turn aside from his studies and planned writing, often to his cost, to combat injustice or misrepresentation, as he saw it, in any form. He was involved.

He rejected, too, a determinant view of history and of human behaviour. Aware of the influence of social, economic and physical forces, interested in human psychology, scientific in his approach to causes, and critical of claims to inspiration, he was nevertheless convinced both of the uncertainties and imponderables in history and of personal influences in decisions. He himself remained an individualist and, on the whole, an optimist. We could learn before it was too late.

This book embodies the essentials of his historical philosophy. That he did not live to elaborate the principles which he had long expounded, to systematise the notes and comments which he had made and to illustrate further the conclusions which he had reached is to be regretted. Many of the views are, indeed, expressed or implicit in one way or another throughout his published works, as well as his correspondence, and especially *The Revolution in Warfare* (1946), *The Defence of the West* (1950), *Deterrent or Defence* (1960) and in successively revised editions of *The Strategy of Indirect Approach* (1948, 1954, 1962).

These essentials changed little over the years. He believed in the importance of the truth that man could, by rational process, discover the truth about himself and about life; that this discovery was without value unless it was expressed and unless its expression resulted in action as well as education. To this end he valued accuracy and lucidity. He valued, perhaps even more, the moral courage to pursue and propagate truths which might be unpopular or detrimental to one's own or other people's immediate interests. He recognized that this discovery could best be fostered under certain political and social conditions which therefore became to him of paramount importance. He was, in the widest sense a liberal while recognizing the limitations, from some points of view, of liberalism.

To what end? He had no faith in blueprints for progress and he sustained the conviction that the end could never justify the means. He was a humane man who believed that human beings, in possession of the facts and undistorted by prejudice, could work out fair solutions for their common problems, based on moderation. Pre-eminently, he applied this philosophy in seeking to understand the causes and restrict the ravages of war.

Other historians have, perhaps, elaborated more impressively comprehensive philosophies. None more fully worked out in his own life, indissolubly merging action and reflection, influence and study, the principles for which he stood.

Adrian J. Liddell Hart

CONTENTS

FOREWORD

If there is any value in such a personal view as I can offer, it is due largely to the fortune of personal circumstances. While in common with the great majority I have had to earn a living, I have had the rare good luck of being able to earn it by trying to discover the truth of events instead of to cover it up, as so many are compelled, against their inclination, by the conditions of their job.

Writing history is a very tough job, and one of the most exhausting. More than any other kind of writing it requires what Sinclair Lewis, in answer to a young man's question, aptly defined as the secret of success: to "make the seat of your pants adhere to the seat of your chair for long enough."

Writing history is also the most exasperating of pursuits. Just as you think you have unraveled a knotty string of evidence, it coils up in a fresh tangle. Moreover you can so easily get caught up or tripped up on some awkward and immovable fact just as you seem to be reaching an irresistible conclusion.

What are the compensations? First, it is a pursuit that has a continual interest and excitement, like an unending detective story in which you are a partaker and not merely a reader.

Secondly, such constant exercise is the best corrective to mental arthritis; the occupational disease of more stereotyped jobs. Third, and above all, it is the least cramping of occupations in a most *vital* respect.

One more point about the writing of history: It should be written in manuscript. Not dictated. It is important always to keep in sight what you have said in the paragraphs before, both for balance and for relationship. And, in each case, both for matter and for style.

I would emphasise a basic value of history to the individual. As Burckhardt said, our deeper hope from experience is that it should "make us, not shrewder (for next time), but wiser (for ever)." History teaches us personal philosophy.

Over two thousand years ago, Polybius, the soundest of ancient historians, began his *History* with the remark that "the most instructive, indeed the only method of learning to bear with dignity the vicissitude of fortune, is to recall the catastrophes of others." History is the best help, being a record of how things usually go wrong.

A long historical view not only helps us to keep calm in a "time of trouble" but reminds us that there is an end to the longest tunnel. Even if we can see no good hope ahead, an historical interest as to what will happen is a help in carrying on. For a thinking man, it can be the strongest check on a suicidal feeling.

I would add that the only hope for humanity, now, is that my particular field of study, warfare, will become purely a subject of antiquarian interest. For with the advent of atomic weapons we have come either to the last page of war, at any rate on the major international scale we have known in the past, or to the last page of history.

B. H. L. H

INTRODUCTION

Man seems to come into the this world with an inalterable belief that he knows best and that he can make others think as he does by force. (How else do we explain why leading men in government madly propose the use of nuclear weapons against the people of another nation because of a trade dispute?) Nations delight in having a militaristic leader represent them and thrive on enforcing their will on lesser powers with a righteous view to the glory and plunder that will follow victory. Peoples are never so united as in the early days of war nor so determined to overcome once they see that a greater effort and more sacrifices will be demanded of them before success is won. All very noble and all fantasy. Has any war in the history of the world followed such a pattern? None on the Ship of Fools ever asks.

We of course, are not on the Ship of Fools, and we do ask. We are those who pursue a knowledge of what happened before our time for pleasure and to gain some understanding that may give us a better judgement in the present and help us better order our lives.

Much has been written on the Theory of History by philosophers and historiologists, but nothing so concise and readable as Liddell Hart's *Why Don't We Learn from History*; the kind of title that makes one wonder and consider. And consider we certainly should in an era when so much bad history and propaganda is being put before us from unknown sources by unknown authors. Publishers no longer employ first rate editors and the peer review process has become a tit for tat affair for career advancement. Education, no longer liberal, has largely become a question of training in some skill to 'qualify' for a job rather than teaching us how to think so as to find our own way. *It is strange how people assume that no training is needed in the pursuit of truth.*[1] We must learn to test and judge the information that comes before us. After all: *Whoever habitually suppresses the truth ... will produce a deformity from the womb of his thought.*

Writing history is a good bit more complex than is generally known. The primary source witnesses historians rely on have neither perfect understanding nor perfect memories of what they relate, their reports contains errors of observation and judgement; further, they tend to evade the truth when friends and superiors are involved. Government reports are frequently written to order for effect, to prove a point, defend a position, or make excusable a failure. Government Official Records, repositories of reports, documents, and such like, are often found to have *lacunæ* and even forgeries. Sensitive or controversial documents go missing or get strangely amended *post facto*.

In times of conflict and for ongoing policy reasons the State issues large numbers of propaganda lies to influence the minds of its citizens in search of support. These officially implanted falsehood are ever after most persistent, even in the face of truth; so persistent that some historians in search of popular readership write false history.

---

1 Italic quotations will be found in Liddell Hart's text below.

The objectivity of any history must therefore be questioned as to the sources selected and how they are used, as to the purpose for writing the history, i.e. popular reading, academic, polemic, etc. Next, who is writing the history and why? Those who write histories start with the handicap of sources, they must also satisfy some overlord or editor. They must select and interpret from an often vast collection of material and present it in a manner that is enjoyable to read. This is not common.

These obstacles mean that any resulting written history is always imperfect and sometimes false. We may think we understand why Caesar marched into Gaul, or why Napoleon marched into Russia, but the causes of twentieth century conflicts are not at all universally understood at this time.

People live by comfortable habit, we think and act more from habit than we do from reflection. Those who read history tend to look for what proves them right and confirms their personal opinions. They defend loyalties. They read with a purpose to affirm or to attack. They resist inconvenient truth and since everyone wants to be on the side of the angels we arrive at a state of mind where we start wars to end wars.

Liddell Hart wrote this little book about military matters, but it's arguments can be extended much more broadly, in fact, to all facets of human life that make use of an accurate knowledge of what went before. Any successful institution, bureaucracy, bank, business, medical, legal, protects itself from change to its own eventual destruction. *For where unification has been able to establish unity of ideas it has usually ended in uniformity, paralysing the growth of new ideas.* It keeps doing what may or may not have at one time worked until it no longer works. Sometimes what is thought to work is no more than a false perception or a theory. And how many times has a method that is known to work been replaced by a theoretical improvement?

Doing the wrong things for the wrong reasons brings us back to the Ship of Fools.

Wide readership of this little book could do much for the betterment of mankind.

Sacramento
Giles Laurén

I. HISTORY AND TRUTH

THE VALUE OF HISTORY

What is the object of history? I would answer, quite simply, "truth." It is a word and an idea that has gone out of fashion. But the results of discounting the possibility of reaching the truth are worse than those of cherishing it.

The object might be more cautiously expressed thus: to find out what happened while trying to find out why it happened. In other words, to seek the causal relations between events.

History has limitations as a *guiding* signpost, however, for although it can show us the right direction, it does not give detailed information about the road conditions.

But its negative value as a *warning* sign is more definite. History can show us what to *avoid,* even if it does not teach us what to do, by showing the most common mistakes that mankind is apt to make and to repeat.

A second object lies in the practical value of history. "Fools," said Bismarck, "say they learn by experience. I prefer to profit by other people's experience."[1] The study of history offers that opportunity in the widest possible measure. It is universal experience, infinitely longer, wider, and more varied than any individual's experience.

How often do people claim superior wisdom on the score of their age and experience. The Chinese especially

---

1 To paraphrase **Aemilius**. Diodorus. XXX. 23.

regard age with veneration, and hold that a man of eighty years or more must be wiser than others. But eighty is nothing for a student of history. There is no excuse for anyone who is not illiterate if he is less than three thousand years old in mind.

The point was well expressed by Polybius. "There are two roads to the reformation for mankind, one through misfortunes of their own, the other through the misfortunes of others; the former is the most unmistakable, the latter the less painful . . . we should always look out for the latter, for thereby we can, without hurt to ourselves, gain a clearer view of the best course to pursue . . . the knowledge gained from the study of true history is the best of all educations for practical life."

The practical value of his advice has been impressed on me in my own particular sphere of study. The main developments that took the General Staffs by surprise in World War I could have been deduced from a study of the successive preceding wars in the previous half century. Why were they not deduced? Partly because the General Staffs' study was too narrow, partly because they were blinded by their own professional interests and sentiments. But the "surprising" developments were correctly deduced from those earlier wars by certain non-official students of war who were able to think with detachment, such as M. Bloch, the Polish banker, and Captain Mayer, the French military writer.

So in studying military problems in the decades after that war I always tried to take a projection from the past through the present into the future. In predicting the decisive developments of World War II I know that I owed more to this practical application of the historical method than to any brain wave of my own.

History is the record of man's steps and slips. It shows us that the steps have been slow and slight; the slips, quick and abounding. It provides us with the opportunity to profit by the stumbles and tumbles of our forerunners. Awareness of our limitations should make us chary of condemning those who made mistakes, but we condemn ourselves if we fail to recognize mistakes.

There is a too common tendency to regard history as a specialist subject; that is the primary mistake. For, on the contrary, history is the essential corrective to all specialisation. Viewed aright, it is the broadest of studies, embracing every aspect of life. It lays the foundation of education by showing how mankind repeats its errors and what those errors are.

THE SIGNIFICANCE OF MILITARY HISTORY

Eighty years ago John Richard Green, in his *History of the English People,* that historical best-seller, delivered the statement "War plays a small part in the real story of European nations, and in that of England its part is smaller than in any." It was an astoundingly unhistorical statement. In the light of today it has a devastating irony.

That view may account for some of our subsequent troubles. For in recent generations, despite the immense growth of research in all other branches of knowledge, the scientific study of war has received too little attention in the universities and too little aid either from them or from government quarters.

The universities' neglect of it had a close connection with the vogue for evolutionary history and economic determinism. Its tendency has been to suggest that movements are independent of individuals and of accident; that "the captains and the kings" count for little; and that the tide of history has flowed on unperturbed by their broils.

Its absurdities are palpable. Can anyone believe that the history of the world would have been the same if the Persians had conquered Greece; if Hannibal had captured Rome; if Caesar had hesitated to cross the Rubicon; if Napoleon had been killed at Toulon? Can anyone believe that England's history would have been unaffected if William of Normandy had been repulsed at Hastings? Or, to come down to recent times, if Hitler had reached Dover instead of stopping at Dunkirk?

The catalogue of cataclysmic happenings, of history-changing "accidents," is endless. But among all the factors which produce sudden changes in the course of history, the issues of war have been the least accidental.

In reality, reason has had a greater influence than fortune on the issue of the wars that have most influenced history. Creative thought has often counted for more than courage; for more, even, than gifted leadership. It is a romantic habit to ascribe to a flash of inspiration in battle what more truly has been due to seeds long sown, to the previous development of some new military practice by the victors, or to avoidable decay in the military practice of the losers.

Unlike those who follow other professions, the "regular" soldier cannot regularly practice his profession. Indeed, it might even be argued that in a literal sense the profession of arms is not a profession at all, but merely "casual employment" and, paradoxically, that it ceased to be a profession when mercenary troops who were employed and paid for the purpose of a war were replaced by standing armies which continued to be paid when there was no war.

If the argument that strictly there is no "profession of arms" will not hold good in most armies today on the score of work, it is inevitably strengthened on the score of practice because major wars have become fewer, though bigger, compared with earlier times. For even the best of peace training is more "theoretical" than "practical" experience.

But Bismarck's often quoted aphorism throws a different and more encouraging light on the problem. It helps us to realize that there are two forms of practical experience, direct and indirect and that, of the two, indirect practical experience may be the more valuable because infinitely wider. Even in the most active career, especially a soldier's career, the scope and possibilities of direct experience are extremely limited. In contrast to the military, the medical profession has incessant practice. Yet the great advances in medicine and surgery have been due more to the scientific thinker and research worker than to the practitioner.

Direct experience is inherently too limited to form an adequate foundation either for theory or for application. At the best it produces an atmosphere that is of value in drying and hardening the structure of thought. The greater value of indirect experience lies in its greater variety and extent. "History is universal experience," the experience not of another but of many others under manifold conditions.

Here is the rational justification for military history as the basis of military education: its preponderant practical value in the training and mental development of a soldier. But the benefit depends, as with all experience, on its breadth, on how closely it approaches the definition quoted above, and on the method of studying it.

Soldiers universally concede the general truth of Napoleon's much quoted dictum that in war "the moral is to the physical as three to one." The actual arithmetical proportion may be worthless, for morale is apt to decline if weapons are inadequate, and the strongest will is of little use if it is inside a dead body. But although the moral and physical factors are inseparable and indivisible, the saying gains its enduring value because it expresses the idea of the predominance of moral factors in all military decisions.

On them constantly turns the issue of war and battle. In the history of war they form the more constant factors, changing only in degree, whereas the physical factors are different in almost every war and every military situation.

THE EXPLORATIONS OF HISTORY

The benefit of history depends, however, on a *broad* view. And that depends on a *wide* study of it To dig deep into one patch is a valuable and necessary training. It is the only way to learn the method of historical research. But when digging deep, it is equally important to get one's bearings by a wide survey. That is essential to appreciate the significance of what one finds, otherwise one is likely "to miss the wood for the trees."

The increasing specialisation of history has tended to decrease the intelligibility of history and thus forfeit the benefit to the community, even the small community of professional historians.

For any historian it is a valuable experience to have lived in the world of affairs and seen bits of history in the making. Not the least part of its value comes through seeing the importance of accidental factors, a touch of liver, a thick head, a sudden tiff, a domestic trouble, or the intervention of the lunch hour.

The understanding of past events is helped by some current experience of how events are determined. It has been my good fortune to see some bits of history in the making, at close quarters, and yet in the position of detachment enjoyed by the onlooker who, according to the proverb, sees most of the game. This experience has taught me that it is often a game of chance, if the fateful effect of a personal dislike, a domestic row, or a bad liver may be counted as accidents. Perhaps the most powerful of such accidental influences on history is the lunch hour.

Observing the working of committees of many kinds, I have long come to realize the crucial importance of lunchtime. Two hours or more may have been spent in deliberate discussion and careful weighing of a problem, but the last quarter of an hour often counts for more than all the rest. At 12:45 p.m. there may be no prospect of an agreed solution, yet around about 1 p.m. important decisions may be reached with little argument, because the attention of the members has turned to watching the hands of their watches. Those moving hands can have a remarkable effect in accelerating the movements of minds to the point of a snap decision. The more influential members of any committee are the most likely to have important lunch engagements, and the more important the committee the more likely is this contingency.

A shrewd committeeman often develops a technique based on this time calculation. He will defer his own intervention in the discussion until lunchtime is near, when the majority of the others are more inclined to accept any proposal that sounds good enough to enable them to keep their lunch engagement. Sometimes he will wait long enough to ensure that formidable opponents have to trickle away before a vote is taken. It was Napoleon who said that an army marches on its stomach. From my observation, I should be inclined to coin a supplementary proverb, that "history marches on the stomachs of statesmen."

That observation applies in more than the time sense. The Japanese locate the seat of courage in the stomach; and such a view is supported by ample evidence from military history of the way that the fighting spirit of troops depends on, and varies with, the state of their stomachs. The source of the passions has also been located in that quarter. All that expresses the extent to which mind and morale depend on the physical, in the normal run of men. And from all that the historian is led to realize how greatly the causation of events on which the fate of nations depends is ruled not by balanced judgment but by momentary currents of feeling, as well as by personal considerations of a low kind.

Another danger, among "hermit" historians, is that they often attach too much value to documents. Men in high office are apt to have a keen sense of their own reputation in history. Many documents are written to deceive or conceal. Moreover, the struggles that go on behind the scenes, and largely determine the issue, are rarely recorded in documents.

Experience has also given me some light into the processes of manufacturing history, artificial history. The product is less transparent than a silk stocking. Nothing can deceive like a document. Here lies the value of the war of 1914-1918 as a training ground for historians. Governments opened their archives, statesmen and generals their mouths, in time to check their records by personal examination of other witnesses. After twenty-years' experience of such work, pure documentary history seems to me akin to mythology.

To those academic historians who still repose faith on it, I have often told a short story with a moral. When the British front was broken in March 1918 and French reinforcements came to help in filling the gap, an eminent French general arrived at a certain army corps headquarters and there majestically dictated orders giving the line on which the troops would stand that night and start their counterattack in the morning. After reading it, with some perplexity, the corps commander exclaimed, "But that line is behind the German front. You lost it yesterday." The great commander, with a knowing smile, thereupon remarked, *"C'est pour l'histoire."* It may be added that for a great part of the war he had held a high staff position where the archives on which such official history would later depend had been under his control.

Many are the gaps to be found in official archives, token of documents destroyed later to conceal what might impair a commander's reputation. More difficult to detect are the forgeries with which some of them have been replaced. On the whole British commanders do not seem to have been capable of more ingenuity than mere destruction or antedating of orders. The French were often more subtle; a general could safeguard the lives of his men as well as his own reputation by writing orders, based on a situation that did not exist, for an attack that nobody carried out, while everybody shared in the credit, since the record went on file.

I have sometimes wondered how the war could be carried on at all when I have found how much of their time some commanders spent in preparing the ground for its historians. If the great men of the past, where the evidence is more difficult to check, were as historically conscious as those of recent generations, it may well be asked what value can be credited to anything more ancient than contemporary history.

The exploration of history is a sobering experience. It reduced the famous American historian, Henry Adams, to the state of cynicism shown in his reply to a questioning letter: "I have written too much history to believe in it. So if anyone wants to differ from me, I am prepared to agree with him." The study of *war* history is especially apt to dispel any illusions about the reliability of men's testimony and their accuracy in general, even apart from the shaping of facts to suit the purposes of propaganda.

Yet if the historian comes to find how hard it is to discover the truth, he may become with practice skilled in detecting untruth, a task which is, by comparison, easier. A sound rule of historical evidence is that while assertions should be treated with critical doubt, admissions are likely to be reliable. If there is one saying that embodies a general truth it is "No man is condemned save out of his own mouth." By applying this test we can go a long way toward a clear verdict on history and on history in the making.

Lloyd George frequently emphasised to me in conversation that one feature that distinguished a first-rate political leader from a second-rate politician is that the former was always careful to avoid making any definite statement that could be subsequently refuted, as he was likely to be caught out in the long run. I gathered from Lloyd George that he learned this lesson in parliamentary experience before 1914.

THE TREATMENT OF HISTORY

An increasing number of modern historians, such as Veronica Wedgwood, have shown that good history and good reading can be blended and thus, by displacing the mythologists, they are bringing history back to the service of humanity. Even so, the academic suspicion of literary style still lingers. Such pedants may well be reminded of the proverb "Hard writing makes easy reading." Such hard writing makes for hard thinking.

Far more effort is required to epitomise facts with clarity than to express them cloudily. Misstatements can be more easily spotted in sentences that are crystal clear than those that are cloudy. The writer has to be more careful if he is not to be caught out. Thus care in writing makes for care in treating the material of history, to evaluate it correctly.

The effort toward deeper psychological analysis is good, so long as perspective is kept. It is equally good that the varnish should be scraped off, so long as the true grain of the character is revealed. It is not so good, except for selling success, when Victorian varnish is replaced by cheap staining, coloured to suit the taste for scandal.

Moreover, the study of personality is apt to be pressed so far that it throws the performance into the background. This certainly simplifies the task of the biographer, who can dispense with the need for a knowledge of the field in which his subject found his life's work. Can we imagine a great statesman without statecraft, a great general without war, a great scientist without science, a great writer without literature; they would look strangely nude. And often commonplace.

A question often debated is whether history is a science *or* an art. The true answer would seem to be that history is a science *and* an art.

The subject must be approached in a scientific spirit of inquiry. Facts must be treated with scientific care for accuracy. But they cannot be interpreted without the aid of imagination and intuition. The sheer *quantity* of evidence is so overwhelming that selection is inevitable. Where there is selection there is art.

Exploration should be objective, but selection is subjective. Its subjectiveness can, and should be, controlled by scientific method and objectiveness. Too many people go to history merely in search of texts for their sermons instead of facts for analysis. But after analysis comes art, to bring out the meaning and to ensure it becomes known.

It was the school of German historians, headed by Ranke, who in the last century started the fashion of trying to be purely scientific. That fashion spread to our own schools of history. Any conclusions or generalisations were shunned, and any well-written books became suspect. What was the result? History became too dull *to read* and devoid of meaning. It became merely a subject *for study* by specialists.

So the void was filled by new myths, of exciting power but appalling consequences. The world has suffered, and Germany worst of all, for the sterilisation of history that started in Germany.

THE SCIENTIFIC APPROACH

Adaptation to changing conditions is the condition of survival. This depends on the simple yet fundamental question of *attitude*. To cope with the problems of the modern world we need, above all, to see them clearly and analyse them scientifically. This requires freedom from prejudice combined with the power of discernment and with a sense of proportion. Only through the capacity to see all relevant factors, to weigh them fairly, and to place them in relation to each other, can we hope to reach an accurately balanced judgment.

Discernment may be primarily a gift, and a sense of proportion, too. But their development can be assisted by freedom from prejudice, which largely rests with the individual to achieve and within his power to achieve it. Or at least to approach it. The way of approach is simple, if not easy, requiring, above all, constant self-criticism and care for precise statement.

It is easier, however, to find an index of progress and consequently of fitness to bear the responsibility of exercising judgment. If a man reads or hears a criticism of anything in which he has an interest, watch whether his first question is as to its fairness and truth. If he reacts to any such criticism with strong emotion; if he bases his complaint on the ground that it is not "in good taste" or that it will have a bad effect, in short, if he shows concern with any question except "Is it true?" he thereby reveals that his own attitude is unscientific.

Likewise if in his turn he judges an idea not on its merits but with reference to the author of it; if he criticizes it as "heresy"; if he argues that authority must be right because it is authority; if he takes a particular criticism as a general depreciation; if he confuses opinion with facts; if he claims that any expression of opinion is "unquestionable"; if he declares that something will "never" come about or is "certain" that any view is right. The path of truth is paved with critical doubt and lighted by the spirit of objective inquiry. To view any question subjectively is self-blinding.

If the study of war in the past has so often proved fallible as a guide to the course and conduct of the next war, it implies not that war is unsuited to scientific study but that the study has not been scientific enough in spirit and method.

It seems hardly possible that the authoritative schools of military thought could have misunderstood as completely as they did the evolution that was so consistently revealed throughout the wars of the nineteenth and early twentieth centuries. A review of the record of error suggests that the only possible explanation is that their study of war was subjective, not objective.

But even if we can reduce the errors of the past in the writing and teaching of military history by soldiers, the fundamental difficulty remains. Faith matters so much to a soldier, in the stress of war, that military training inculcates a habit of unquestioning obedience which in turn fosters an unquestioning acceptance of the prevailing doctrine. While fighting is a most practical test of theory, it is a small part of soldiering; and there is far more in soldiering that tends to make men the slaves of a theory.

Moreover, the soldier must have faith in his power to defeat the enemy; hence to question, even on material grounds, the possibility of successful attack is a risk to faith. Doubt is unnerving save to philosophic minds, and armies are not composed of philosophers, either at the top or at the bottom. In no activity is optimism so necessary to success, for it deals so largely with the unknown, even unto death. The margin that separates optimism from blind folly is narrow. Thus there is no cause for surprise that soldiers have so often overstepped it and become the victims of their faith.

The soldier could hardly face the test defined in the motto of the famous Lung Ming Academy, a motto that headed each page of the books used there: "The student must first learn to approach the subject in a spirit of doubt." The point had been still more clearly expressed in the eleventh-century teaching of Chang-Tsai: "If you can doubt at points where other people feel no impulse to doubt, then you are making progress."

THE FEAR OF TRUTH

We learn from history that in every age and every clime the majority of people have resented what seems in retrospect to have been purely matter-of-fact comment on their institutions. We learn too that nothing has aided the persistence of falsehood, and the evils resulting from it, more than the unwillingness of good people to admit the truth when it was disturbing to their comfortable assurance. Always the tendency continues to be shocked by natural comment and to hold certain things too "sacred" to think about.

I can conceive of no finer ideal of a man's life than to face life with clear eyes instead of stumbling through it like a blind man, an imbecile, or a drunkard, which, in a thinking sense, is the common preference. How rarely does one meet anyone whose first reaction to anything is to ask "Is it true?" Yet unless that is a man's natural reaction it shows that truth is not uppermost in his mind, and, unless it is, true progress is unlikely.

The most dangerous of all delusions are those that arise from the adulteration of history in the imagined interests of national and military morale. Although this lesson of experience has been the hardest earned, it remains the hardest to learn. Those who have suffered most show their eagerness to suffer more.

In 1935 a distinguished German general contributed to the leading military organ of his country an article entitled "Why Can't We Camouflage?" It was not, as might be supposed, an appeal to revive and develop the art of deceiving the eye with the object of concealing troop movements and positions. The camouflage which the

author wished to see adopted in the German Army was the
concealment of the less pleasing facts of history. He
deplored the way that, after World War I, the diplomatic
documents of the Wilhelmstrasse were published in full,
even to the Kaiser's marginal comments. The general
concluded his appeal for the use of camouflage in the
sphere of history by recalling "the magnificent English
dictum '*Wahr ist was wirkt.*' (Anything that works is true.)

The student of military history may be surprised not at
the plea but that the general should appear to regard it as
novel. History that bears the qualification "official" carries
with it a natural reservation; and the additional prefix
"military" is apt to imply a double reservation. The history
of history yields ample evidence that the art of camouflage
was developed in that field long before it was applied to
the battlefield.

This camouflaged history not only conceals faults and
deficiencies that could otherwise be remedied, but
engenders false confidence, and false confidence underlies
most of the failures that military history records. It is the
dry rot of armies. But its effects go wider and are felt
earlier. For the false confidence of military leaders has
been a spur to war.

THE EVASION OF TRUTH

We learn from history that men have constantly echoed
the remark ascribed to Pontius Pilate: "What is truth?" And
often in circumstances that make us wonder why. It is
repeatedly used as a smoke screen to mask a manoeuvre,
personal or political, and to cover an evasion of the issue.
It may be a justifiable question in the deepest sense. Yet
the longer I watch current events, the more I have come to

see how many of our troubles arise from the habit, on all sides, of suppressing or distorting what we know quite well is the truth, out of devotion to a cause, an ambition, or an institution; at bottom, this devotion being inspired by our own interest.

The history of 1914-1918 is full of examples. Passchendaele perhaps provides the most striking. It is clear from what Haig said beforehand that his motive was a desire to, and belief that he could, win the war single-handed in 1917 by a British offensive in Flanders before the Americans arrived. By the time he was ready to launch it all the conditions had changed, and the chief French commanders expressed grave doubts. Yet in his eagerness to persuade a reluctant British Cabinet to allow him to fulfil his dream, he disclosed none of the unfavourable facts which were known to him and exaggerated those that seemed favourable. When his offensive was launched on the last day of July, it failed completely on the part that was most vital. Yet he reported to London that the results were "most satisfactory." The weather broke that very day and the offensive became bogged.

When the Prime Minister, becoming anxious at the mounting toll of casualties, went over to Flanders, Haig argued that the poor physique of the prisoners then being taken was proof that his offensive was reducing the German Army to exhaustion. When the Prime Minister asked to see one of the prisoners' cages, one of Haig's staff telephoned in advance to give instructions that "all able-bodied prisoners were to be removed from the corps cages" before his arrival. The chain of deception continued, and the offensive went on until 400,000 men had been sacrificed.

In later years Haig was wont to argue in excuse that his offensive had been undertaken at the behest of the French and that "the possibility of the French Army breaking up compelled me to go on attacking." But in his letters at the time, since revealed, he declared that its morale was "excellent." And the following spring he blamed the Government when his own army, thus brought to the verge of physical and moral exhaustion, failed to withstand the German offensive.

Haig was an honourable man according to his lights, but his lights were dim. The consequences which have made "Passchendaele" a name of ill-omen may be traced to the combined effect of his tendency to deceive himself; his tendency, therefore, to encourage his subordinates to deceive him; and their "loyal" tendency to tell a superior what was likely to coincide with his desires. Passchendaele is an object lesson in this kind of well-meaning, if not disinterested, untruthfulness.

As a young officer I had cherished a deep respect for the Higher Command, but I was sadly disillusioned about many of them when I came to see them more closely from the angle of a military correspondent. It was saddening to discover how many apparently honourable men would stoop to almost anything to help their own advancement.

One of the commanders who cultivated my acquaintance assiduously, Montgomery-Massingberd,[1] asked me to collaborate with him in writing a book on the

---

1 Field Marshal Sir Archibald Montgomery-Massingberd.

lessons of the war, and when we went out to study the battlefields together, I found that he evaded every awkward point and soon I came to realize that his underlying purpose in proposing such a book was to show how brilliant and unblemished had been the operation of the Fourth Army, of which he had been Chief of Staff. So I excused myself from assisting in that piece of advertisement. He also, I found, had a habit of dropping in my ear detrimental insinuations about other generals who happened to be competitors with him in climbing the military ladder.

He eventually reached the top of it, though not with my assistance, and his tenure of the post was marked by the worst period of stagnation in the Army's progress between the wars. That was all the more unfortunate because he came into office as Chief of the Imperial General Staff just as Hitler was taking over power in Germany. When Ironside became CIGS on the outbreak of war in 1939 and contemplated the list of the deficiencies in the Army's equipment, he was so appalled that he pointed to the portraits of Montgomery-Massingberd and his predecessor, Milne, in his office and vehemently exclaimed, "Those are the two men mainly responsible, they ought to be taken out and shot." (That verdict was too hard on Milne.)

A different habit, with worse effect, was the way that ambitious officers when they came in sight of promotion to the generals' list, would decide that they would bottle up their thoughts and ideas, as a safety precaution, until they reached the top and could put these ideas into practice. Unfortunately the usual result, after years of such self-repression for the sake of their ambition, was that when the bottle was eventually uncorked the contents had evaporated.

I found that moral courage was quite as rare in the top levels of the services as among politicians. It was also a surprise to me to find that those who had shown the highest degree of physical courage tended to be those who were most lacking in moral courage, and the clue to this seemed to be largely in the growing obsession with personal career ambition, particularly in the cases where an unhappy home life resulted in an inordinate concern with career prospects. The other main cause in diminishing moral courage, however, was a lack of private means that led commanding officers to wilt before their superiors because of concern with the problem of providing for their children's education. That factor was very marked in the German generals' submissiveness to Hitler, and this became the more understandable to me because I had seen it operate in Britain in much less difficult circumstances.

I have been fortunate, as I remarked in the preface of my *Memoirs,* in being a "free lance," often officially consulted but never officially employed or subsidised, and thus having no "interest to pursue" or "ax to grind" in seeking the truth and expressing my views objectively. In my experience the troubles of the world largely come from excessive regard to other interests.

BLINDING LOYALTIES

We learn from history that those who are disloyal to their own superiors are most prone to preach loyalty to their subordinates. Not many years ago there was a man who preached it so continually when in high position as to make it a catchword; that same man had been privately characterized by his chief, his colleague, and his assistant in earlier years as one who would swallow anything in order to get on.

Loyalty is a noble quality, so long as it is not blind and does not exclude the higher loyalty to truth and decency. But the word is much abused. For "loyalty," analysed, is too often a polite word for what would be more accurately described as "a conspiracy for mutual inefficiency." In this sense it is essentially selfish, like a servile loyalty, demeaning both to master and servant. They are in a false relation to each other, and the loyalty which is then so much prized can be traced, if we probe deep enough, to an ultimate selfishness on either side. "Loyalty" is not a quality we can isolate; so far as it is real, and of intrinsic value, it is implicit in the possession of other virtues.

These minor loyalties also invade the field of history and damage its fruits. The search for truth for truth's sake is the mark of the historian. To that occupation many are called but few are worthy, not necessarily for want of gifts but for lack of the urge or the resolution to follow the gleam wherever it may lead. Too many have sentimental encumbrances, even if they are not primarily moved, as so often happens in the field of historical biography, by the sentiment of kinship, or of friendship, or of discipleship. On a lower plane come those who suit their conclusions to the taste of an audience or a patron.

Deep is the gulf between works of history as written and the truth of history, and perhaps never more so than in books dealing with military history. If one reason is that these are usually written by soldiers untrained as historians and another that there is frequently some personal link, whether of acquaintance or tradition, between author and subject, a deeper reason lies in a habit of mind. For the soldier, "My country, right or wrong" must be the watchword. And this essential loyalty, whether it be to a country, to a regiment, or to comrades, is so ingrained in him that when he passes from action to reflection it is difficult for him to acquire instead the historian's single-minded loyalty to the truth.

Not that the most impartial historian is ever likely to attain truth in its entirety; but he is likely to approach it more closely if he has this single-mindedness. For the historian loyal to his calling it would be impossible to put forward the suggestion, such as one heard from distinguished participants in war, that certain episodes might "best be glossed over" in war histories. Yet these officers were men of indisputable honour and quite unconscious that they were sinning not only against the interests of their country's future but against truth, the essential foundation for honour.

The effect was all too strikingly illustrated in the case of the man who was in charge of the British official military histories of World War I, General Edmonds. In the detective side of historian-ship, as well as in background knowledge, he was outstandingly well qualified for the task. In the early years of the task he often said that he could not state the damaging truth in an official history because of loyalty to the service and to his old comrades among the generals, yet wanted to make it known privately to other historians, which he did. But as time passed and he grew older, he gradually hypnotised himself into the belief that the gloss he felt bound to put over the facts was the truth, the core of the matter and not merely the protective covering.

That practice became a fatal hindrance to the chance of getting the lessons of World War I clear in time for the next generation to profit by them in World War II. Historical writers who are free from official attachments and institutional obligations should count themselves fortunate in being unfettered, rather than priding themselves on an innate personal superiority of honesty.

Truth may not be absolute, but it is certain that we are likely to come nearest to it if we search for it in a purely scientific spirit and analyse the facts with a complete detachment from all loyalties save that to truth itself.

It implies that one must be ready to discard one's own pet ideas and theories as the search progresses.

In no field has the pursuit of truth been more difficult than that of military history. Apart from the way that the facts were hidden, the need for technical knowledge tended to limit the undertaking to trained soldiers, and these were not trained in historical methods.

Moreover, the military hierarchy showed a natural anxiety lest a knowledge of the fallibility of the generals of yesterday should disturb the young soldier's trust in his generals of today and tomorrow. A realisation of the cycle of familiar errors, endlessly recurring, which largely makes up the course of military history may lead one to think that the only hope of escape lies in a more candid scrutiny of past experience and a new honesty in facing the facts.

But one should still be able to appreciate the point of view of those who fear the consequences. Faith matters so much in times of crisis. One must have gone deep into history before reaching the conviction that truth matters more.

II. GOVERNMENT AND FREEDOM
BLINDFOLDED AUTHORITY

All of us do foolish things, but the wiser realize what they do. The most dangerous error is failure to recognize our own tendency to error. That failure is a common affliction of authority.

From many examples may be cited one from World War I. When reports percolated to Paris about the neglected state of the Verdun defences, Joffre was asked for an assurance that they would be improved. In reply he indignantly denied that there was any cause for anxiety and demanded the names of those who had dared to suggest it: "I cannot be a party to soldiers under my command bringing before the Government, by channels other than the hierarchic channel, complaints or protests about the execution of my orders. ... It is calculated to disturb profoundly the spirit of discipline in the Army."

That reply might well be framed and hung up in all the bureaus of officialdom the world over to serve as the mummy at the feast. For within two months his doctrine of infallibility collapsed like a punctured balloon, with tragic effects for his army. But here, as so often happens, personal retribution was slow and ironical in its course. The man who had given warning was to be one of the first victims of its neglect, while Joffre for a time gained fresh popular laurels from the heroic sacrifice by which complete disaster was averted.

The pretence to infallibility is instinctive in a hierarchy. But to understand the cause is not to underrate the harm that the pretence has produced, in every sphere.

We learn from history that the critics of authority have always been rebuked in self-righteous tones, if no worse fate has befallen them, yet have repeatedly been justified by history. To be "agin the Government" may be a more philosophic attitude than it appears. For the tendency of all "governments" is to infringe the standards of decency and truth; this is inherent in their nature and hardly avoidable in their practice.

Hence the duty of the good citizen who is free from the responsibility of Government is to be a watchdog upon it, lest Government impair the fundamental objects which it exists to serve. It is a necessary evil, thus requiring constant watchfulness and check.

RESTRAINTS OF DEMOCRACY

We learn from history that democracy has commonly put a premium on conventionality. By its nature, it prefers those who keep step with the slowest march of thought and frowns on those who may disturb the "conspiracy for mutual inefficiency." Thereby, this system of government tends to result in the triumph of mediocrity, and entails the exclusion of first-rate ability if this is combined with honesty. But the alternative to it, despotism, almost inevitably means the triumph of stupidity. And of the two evils, the former is the less.

Hence it is better that ability should consent to its own sacrifice, and subordination to the regime of mediocrity, rather than assist in establishing a regime where, in the light of past experience, brute stupidity will be enthroned and ability may only preserve its footing at the price of dishonesty.

What is of value in "England" and "America" and worth defending is its tradition of freedom, the guarantee of its vitality. Our civilization, like the Greek, has, for all its blundering way, taught the value of freedom, of criticism of authority, and of harmonising this with order. Anyone who urges a different system, for efficiency's sake, is betraying the vital tradition.

The experience of the two-party system developed in English politics, and transplanted across the ocean, continued long enough to show its practical superiority, whatever its theoretical drawbacks, to any other system of government that has yet been tried. I cannot see that socialism (in the "true" sense of the term) can be attained and made secure without tending to its logical end, the totalitarian state. It is not productive basically of a good or an efficient community. In England, at any rate, it has carried on, and no more, the improvement of the conditions of the "underdog" that was developed, above all, by Lloyd George.

POWER POLITICS IN A DEMOCRACY

The part that power plays in relations between nations is coming to be better understood and more generally recognized than it was in a more optimistic period. The term "power politics" is now in such common usage as to represent an admission of reality. But there is still a lack of public understanding as to where power lies and how it is exercised within a nation.

In a democratic system, power is entrusted to committees. These are the main organs of the body politic on all levels, from local councils up to the highest committees of Government. But the process by which decisions are reached is very different in reality from what is conceived in constitutional theory. Moreover, issues are apt to be powerfully influenced by factors which have no relation to principles and of which theory takes little account.

While committee meetings are not so frequently held in the late afternoon as in the morning, dinner itself provides both an opportunity and an atmosphere suited to the informal kind of committee that tends to be more influential than those which are formally constituted. The informal type is usually small, and the smaller it is the more influential it may be. The "two or three gathered together" may outweigh a formal committee of twenty or thirty members to which it may often be related "under the blanket," where it is assembled by someone who has a leading voice in the larger official committee. For it will represent his personal selection in the way of consultants, and, its members being chosen for their congeniality as well as for their advisory value, it is likely to reach clear-cut conclusions, which in turn may be translated into the decisions of a formal committee.

For in any gathering of twenty or thirty men there is likely to be so much diversity and nebulosity of views that the consent of the majority can generally be gained for any conclusion that is sufficiently definite, impressively backed by well-considered arguments, and sponsored by a heavyweight member, especially if the presentation is carefully stage-managed.

The most significant example of this dinner-table influence is to be found on the highest level, which in Britain is the Cabinet. This first became apparent to me years ago when I happened to know rather closely two men who held the office of Secretary of State for the same department in successive Governments and found that while the first dined with the Prime Minister only occasionally, and then usually at rather large dinner parties, the second dined with the Prime Minister every few days, either alone or with only one or two other intimate friends present. Then I noticed the difference between the "deal" which the department received in the one case compared with the other and also the way that the second man influenced Government decisions on many matters outside his own departmental sphere. Later observation brought more indications to the same effect.

The "Sea Lords" of the Admiralty played a large part at the dinner tables of London society before World War II. That "dining out" power weighed more than any weapon power in securing for the Navy the largest share of the national defence budget, although less successful in fending off the interference of the German Air Force when war came. Across the dinner table before the war they were always confident that battleships could operate without serious risk from air attack, but when the test came, in war, they were compelled to revise their opinion after suffering heavy losses.

The Cabinet in England is in constitutional theory the decisive organ of the state; the brain of the national body. But it is a big committee, too big to be really effective as a source of decisions. A realisation of that fact has led to repeated efforts toward a reduction of its size. Most of these efforts have resulted in no more than a paring down of numbers, in order to keep the membership nearer the figure of twenty than thirty. Those minor reductions could make no essential difference. A committee of twenty is no better than a committee of thirty for the airing of views, while in either case the decisions are almost bound to be guided by conclusions previously formulated in a smaller circle. The nearest approach to an effective organ was the "War Cabinet" of five which Lloyd George formed in 1917 to deal with the critical situation then existing. It was a Cabinet within a Cabinet. The system was reintroduced by Churchill in World War II.

There is always an "Inner Cabinet," but usually it has no official constitution and might be more aptly described as an "Intimate Cabinet." It is a fluid body. It may comprise those members of the actual Cabinet on whom the Prime Minister mainly relies or considers it essential to consult. But it may include men who have no ministerial position. For its constituent elements depend on the Prime Minister's judgment, and choice, of the men whose opinions are most helpful and stimulating to him. The essential condition of membership is intimacy, not status.

In the private discussions of this small circle matters of high policy are debated and decisions often crystallised in advance of a Cabinet meeting which may, in effect, be no more than a means of ratifying them. Such a procedure may appear unconstitutional, yet it is quite proper so long as the Prime Minister subsequently explains his proposals to his Cabinet colleagues at one of these formal meetings and secures their endorsement. That is rarely difficult, because of the Prime Minister's natural ascendency in the Cabinet, coupled with his initial advantage in having his arguments already prepared.

The more powerful his own personality, as a reinforcement to his status, the more easily he can procure a smooth passage for his proposals. If he anticipates a difficulty, he can often forestall it by a preliminary talk in private with the most weighty of his colleagues. In most cases he can reckon on the acquiescence of the bulk of them in any course that he propounds. A Prime Minister who comes to a Cabinet meeting with his mind made up, and a plan thought out, is not likely to be thwarted, nor even seriously opposed. All that is quite natural and quite in order.

In a realistic view, the important links in the chain of causation are the earlier ones, the influence which led the Prime Minister to make up his mind. There lies the significance of his intimate circle of consultants, with whom he is accustomed to discuss affairs and from whom he draws ideas. They, together with the Prime Minister, are the real moulders of policy.

Besides being his private advisers, they often act as a discreet intelligence and liaison service. They may be used to carry out confidential inquiries and keep him in touch with what other people are thinking. They may also be entrusted with delicate missions at home or abroad, to take soundings prior to any official approach.

In the various departments a similar process could be traced, especially in those where power ostensibly rests with a council. Major matters that came before the Board of Admiralty, the Army Council, or the Air Council had often in reality been decided beforehand in private discussion between the Minister and the chief service members or the Permanent Secretary. But where the Minister was a strong personality with a mind of his own, he might be more inclined to formulate his own policy with the help of one or more intimate advisers on whom he relied to provide him with a detached and disinterested opinion.

That practice merely repeats what is constantly seen in the business world, where the chairman of a company is apt to be more influenced by one or two individuals than by the collective mind of the directors who consider the policy presented to them. In matters of policy a board meeting may modify as well as ratify, but of its nature it is not suited to originate.

MEN BEHIND THE SCENES

The "intimate advisers" of a Prime Minister, a President, or, in turn, of a departmental head rarely become known to the public in that capacity, though their influence may be guessed, discussed, and criticised in the higher official circles. When they are already well known in their own right, they are often more handicapped, since their influence is apt to excite more suspicion and jealousy. That handicap applies not only to outside advisers but also, and even more, to such advisers as hold ministerial offices or Civil Service posts below the top level.

Before and early in World War I one of the most widely influential intimate advisers was Lord Esher. He never held high office, but achieved a record in the number of offers he declined, including the offices of Secretary of

State for War and Viceroy of India. He derived much of his back-stage influence from the extent to which he was in the confidence of King Edward VII and King George V in turn, as well as of leading ministers. Another notable veiled figure of that period was J. A. Spender, the editor of the Westminster Gazette. It was often remarked that the news columns of his paper were strangely backward in anticipating developments; the explanation being that he himself was so closely in the confidence of the Prime Minister that his knowledge of what was going to happen became a stifling gag on his power to fulfil his editorial function.

At the time of the second Labor Government Lord Thomson, the Air Minister, had an influence on the Prime Minister, Ramsay MacDonald, much greater than his Cabinet position and extending into spheres beyond the limits of his departmental office. After Thomson was killed in the disaster to the airship R.101, John Buchan became an intimate adviser of Ramsay MacDonald and a link with the leader of the Conservative party, Baldwin in the coalition period. After Baldwin again became Prime Minister, the personal association between him and Mr. J. C. C. Davidson appeared to become an important factor in shaping Government policy. In the last two years of Mr. Baldwin's regime, Sir Horace Wilson, who had been chief industrial adviser since 1930, was "seconded to the Treasury for service with the Prime Minister." He acquired still greater influence when Neville Chamberlain became Prime Minister in 1937, and exercised it over the whole field of policy, including foreign affairs. Ministers frequently complained that they were unable to see the

Prime Minister on important matters but had to put them through to Sir Horace Wilson and get decisions that way.

When Churchill became Prime Minister in 1940 the importance of Brendan Bracken and Lord Beaverbrook in his counsels became widely known. He also brought with him Professor Lindemann, later Lord Cherwell, whose advisory position was regularised by the official announcement of his appointment as the Prime Minister's "personal assistant." Major Desmond Morton was another.

Though the practical value of such intimate advisers has become increasingly accepted, they have remained more in the background in Britain than in the United States. There, during World War I, Edward M. House was much more than the right hand of President Wilson; he was the "other half," and although he never held office he often deputised for the President at inter-Allied conferences. In World War II, Harry Hopkins played almost as big a part as President Roosevelt's representative, as well as his most intimate and constant adviser.

PATTERN OF DICTATORSHIP

We learn from history that self-made despotic rulers follow a standard pattern.

In gaining power:

They exploit, consciously or unconsciously, a state of popular dissatisfaction with the existing regime or of hostility between different sections of the people.

They attack the existing regime violently and combine their appeal to discontent with unlimited promises (which, if successful, they fulfil only to a limited extent).

They claim that they want absolute power for only a short time (but "find" subsequently that the time to relinquish it never comes).

They excite popular sympathy by presenting the picture of a conspiracy against them and use this as a lever to gain a firmer hold at some crucial stage.

On gaining power:

They soon begin to rid themselves of their chief helpers, "discovering" that those who brought about the new order have suddenly become traitors to it.

They suppress criticism on one pretext or another and punish anyone who mentions facts which, however true, are unfavourable to their policy.

They enlist religion on their side, if possible, or, if its leaders are not compliant, foster a new kind of religion subservient to their ends.

They spend public money lavishly on material works of a striking kind, in compensation for the freedom of spirit and thought of which they have robbed the public.

They manipulate the currency to make the economic position of the state appear better than it is in reality.

They ultimately make war on some other state as a means of diverting attention from internal conditions and allowing discontent to explode outward.

They use the rallying cry of patriotism as a means of riveting the chains of their personal authority more firmly on the people.

They expand the superstructure of the state while undermining its foundations by breeding sycophants at the expense of self-respecting collaborators, by appealing to the popular taste for the grandiose and sensational instead of true values, and by fostering a romantic instead of a realistic view, thus ensuring the ultimate collapse, under their successors if not themselves, of what they have created.

This political confidence trick, itself a familiar string of tricks, has been repeated all down the ages. Yet it rarely fails to take in a fresh generation.

THE PSYCHOLOGY OF DICTATORSHIP

We learn from history that time does little to alter the psychology of dictatorship. The effect of power on the mind of the man who possesses it, especially when he has gained it by successful aggression, tends to be remarkably similar in every age and in every country.

It is worthwhile to retrace the course of Napoleon's Russian campaign, not so much for the detail of operations, but as an object lesson in the workings of a dictator's mind. For this purpose we can profit, in particular, from a study of the memoirs of Caulaincourt, who not only took part in the march to Moscow but was Napoleon's chosen companion on the journey back, after Napoleon had left his army to its fate.

The adventure which undermined Napoleon's domination of Europe and brought his New Order crashing to the ground was directly due to his mingled dissatisfaction and uneasiness over Russia's attitude toward his plans for subduing England, the last obstacle to his path to world domination. In Napoleon's eyes, the Tsar's attempt to moderate the burden of the Continental system appeared the thin edge of a wedge that would disjoint the lever on which he was relying to weaken England's stubborn refusal to negotiate.

Although Napoleon had himself permitted modifications in the system where it happened to pinch the French, he expected his allies, as well as the occupied countries, to put up with privations without mitigation in his interest. And in rigid fulfilment of that fundamentally irrational logic he now took the decision to impose his will on Russia by force of arms. He decided on this course against the advice of his closest and wisest counsellors.

By the middle of June 1812 he had assembled an army of 450,000 men, a vast size for those times, on the Russian frontier between the Baltic Sea and the Pripet Marshes. At ten o'clock on the night of June 23 the pontoon detachments threw their bridges across the Niemen and the crossing began. Napoleon's mood was expressed in his remark to Caulaincourt: "In less than two months' time, Russia will be suing for peace."

On approaching Vilna, Napoleon found that the Russians had abandoned the city. "It was truly heartbreaking for him to have to give up all hope of a great battle before Vilna and he voiced his bitterness by crying out upon the cowardice of his foes."

After five weeks' campaigning, despite his deep advance, he had inflicted little damage on the enemy, while his own army had been reduced by at least a third in numbers and still more in efficiency.

As Caulaincourt tells us: "He believed there would be battle because he wanted one, and he believed that he should win it, because it was essential that he should." So he was led to advance on Smolensk. On entering the charred and deserted city, Napoleon gained a fresh access of confidence, declaring: "Before a month is out, we shall be in Moscow; in six weeks we shall have peace."

On September 14 Napoleon reached Moscow and found that the Russians had evacuated the city. That evening fire broke out in many quarters, and the greater part of the city was soon in flames.

This destruction of Moscow by the Russians sobered Napoleon. He became anxious to seek any chance of peace. But he was still incapable of understanding the bitterness he had aroused. As a result he prolonged his stay in burnt-out Moscow in the misplaced hope that the Russians would the more quickly respond to his overtures. Instead, these were regarded, rightly, as evidence of his growing embarrassment. On October 25 he reluctantly gave orders to begin the march back to Smolensk.

By the time Smolensk was reached, on November 9, the army had shrunk to a bare 50,000. On reaching the Beresina the army barely escaped complete disaster, and after reaching Smorgoni Napoleon decided to leave his army and dash back to Paris, to raise fresh forces and to be on the spot where his presence would restore confidence when the news of the disastrous end of the Russian campaign reached the people of France and the watchful capitals of conquered Europe.

He talked at length of the defects and deficiencies of his various assistants, and on one of them, Talleyrand, he made a comment that cast its shadow nearer home: "Once you've behaved like a knave, you must never behave like a fool."

To the unromantic historian, Napoleon is more of a knave than a hero. But to the philosopher, he is even more of a fool than a knave. His folly was shown in the ambition he conceived and the goal he pursued, while his frustration was ensured by his capacity to fool himself. Yet the reflection remains that such a fool and his devastating folly are largely the creation of smaller, if better, fools. So great is the fascination of romantic folly!

We learn that when Napoleon visited the bivouacs of his frozen and starving soldiers, before he left them, he "passed through the crowds of these unfortunates without a murmur being heard. They blamed the weather and uttered not a word of reproach about the pursuit of glory." And in the end he went back home in comparative comfort to receive the congratulations of his subjects on his safe return and to collect among them fresh reserves of cannon fodder with which to set out afresh on the pursuit of glory.

Almost exactly 129 years after Napoleon launched his invasion of Russia, Hitler began his attack on Russia, on June 22, 1941. Despite the revolutionary changes which had taken place in the interval he was to provide a tragic demonstration of the truth that mankind, and least of all its "great men," do not learn from history.

THE BASIC FLAW IN DICTATORSHIP

It would be untruthful not to recognize that authoritarian regimes, such as Napoleon's, have produced some good fruits. They are to be found in both the material and the spiritual fields. Many social reforms and practical improvements have been carried out in a few years which a democracy would have debated for generations. A dictator's interest and support may be won for public works, artistic activities, and archaeological explorations in which a parliamentary government would not be interested because they promise no votes.

It is also to the credit of the totalitarian systems that they have stimulated service to the community and the sense of comradeship, up to a point. In this respect their effect on a nation is like that of war. And, as in war, the quick-ripening good fellowship of the powerless many is apt to obscure the intrigues of the powerful few, the withering of the roots in such a soil, and the gradual decay of the tree. Bad means lead to no good end.

Their own declarations of faith are the truest test of the authoritarian regimes. In weighing the wrongs there is no need to argue over particular cases, which the victims assert and they often deny, because they proudly avow an attitude which makes such instances inherently probable.

It is man's power of thought which has generated the current of human progress through the ages. Thus the thinking man must be against authoritarianism in any form, because it shows its fear of thoughts which do not suit momentary authority.

Any sincere writer must be against it, because it believes in censorship.

Any true historian must be against it, because he can see that it leads to the repetition of old follies, as well as to the deliberate adulteration of history.

Anyone who tries to solve problems scientifically must be against it, since it refuses to recognize that criticism is the life blood of science.

In sum, any seeker of truth must be against it, because it subordinates truth to state expediency. This spells stagnation.

But "anti-Fascism" or "anti-Communism" is not enough. Nor is even the defence of freedom. What has been gained may not be maintained, against invasion without and erosion within, if we are content to stand still. The peoples who are partially free as a result of what their forebears achieved in the seventeenth, eighteenth, and nineteenth centuries must continue to spread the gospel of freedom and work for the extension of the conditions, social and economic as well as political, which are essential to make men free.

DISTURBING TRENDS

Looking at the situation today in Britain, America, and other democratic countries, compared with the past, and from a more detached point of view, it seems to me that, while there has been an improvement in some respects, handicaps have increased in other ways, and on balance these may be worse.

One factor is an excessive growth of "security-mindedness," more bureaucratic than realistic, so that it is often carried to ludicrous extremes. It is certainly more difficult for Parliament (or Congress) to acquire the knowledge on which to base useful comment on defence matters. Another factor, related to the first, is the growth of "P.R.-mindedness," and this particularly affects comment by serving officers.

The articles that Fuller[1] and I wrote about existing defects and new developments often caused trouble in the War Office and earned us disfavour, but officialdom stopped short of forbidding publication. Now the heretical

---

1 Major General J. F. C. Fuller.

ideas we expressed have become orthodox, but anyone who attempted a fresh bound in ideas and a fresh look into the future might find it more difficult to obtain permission to publish such ideas, or criticism of the existing doctrine.

THE FALLACY OF COMPULSION

We learn from history that the compulsory principle always breaks down in practice. It is practicable to prevent men doing something; moreover that principle of restraint, or regulation, is essentially justifiable in so far as its application is needed to check interference with others' freedom. But it is not, in reality, possible to make men do something without risking more than is gained from the compelled effort. The method may appear practicable, because it often works when applied to those who are merely hesitant. When applied to those who are definitely unwilling it fails, however, because it generates friction and fosters subtle forms of evasion that spoil the effect which is sought. The test of whether a principle works is to be found in the product.

Efficiency springs from enthusiasm, because this alone can develop a dynamic impulse. Enthusiasm is incompatible with compulsion, because it is essentially spontaneous. Compulsion is thus bound to deaden enthusiasm, because it dries up the source. The more an individual, or a nation, has been accustomed to freedom, the more deadening will be the effect of a change to compulsion.

Many years spent in the study of war, a study which gradually went beyond its current technique to its wellsprings, changed my earlier and conventional belief in the value of conscription. It brought me to see that the compulsory principle was fundamentally inefficient and the conscription method out of date, a method that clung, like the ivy, to quantitative standards in an age when the trend of warfare was becoming increasingly qualitative. For it sustained the fetish of mere numbers at a time when skill and enthusiasm were becoming ever more necessary for the effective handling of the new weapons.

Conscription does not fit the conditions of modern warfare; its specialised technical equipment, mobile operations, and fluid situations. Success increasingly depends on individual initiative, which in turn springs from a sense of personal responsibility; these senses are atrophied by compulsion. Moreover, every unwilling man is a germ carrier, spreading infection to an extent altogether disproportionate to the value of the service he is forced to contribute.

Looking still further into the question, and thinking deeper, I came to see, also, that the greatest contributory factor to the great wars which had racked the world in recent generations had been the conscription system.

These logical deductions are confirmed by analysis of historical experience. The modern system of military conscription was born in France; it was, ironically, the misbegotten child of Revolutionary enthusiasm. Within a generation its application had become so obnoxious that its abolition was the primary demand of the French people following Napoleon's downfall. Meanwhile, however, it had been transplanted to more suitable soil in Prussia. And just over half a century later the victories that Prussia gained led to the resurrection of conscription in France. Its reimposition was all the easier because the renewed autocracy of Napoleon III had accustomed the French people to the interference and constraints of bureaucracy. In the generation that followed, the revival of the spirit of freedom in France was accompanied by a growth of the petty bureaucracy, parasites feeding on the body politic. From this, the French could never succeed in shaking free; and in their efforts they merely developed corruption, which is the natural consequence of an ineffective effort to loosen the grip of compulsion by evasion.

It is generally recognized today that this rampant growth of bureaucratically induced corruption was the dry rot of the Third Republic. But on deeper examination the cause can be traced further back, to the misunderstanding of their own principles which led a section of the creators of the French Revolution to adopt a method fundamentally opposed to their fulfilment.

It might be thought that conscription should be less detrimental to the Germans, since they are more responsive to regulation and have no deeply rooted tradition of freedom. Nevertheless, it is of significance that the Nazi movement was essentially a voluntary movement, exclusive rather than comprehensive, and that the most important sections of the German forces, the air force and the task force, were recruited on a semi-voluntary basis. There is little evidence to suggest that the ordinary "mass" of the German Army had anything like the same enthusiasm, and considerable evidence to suggest that this conscripted mass constituted a basic weakness in Germany's apparent strength.

The system, as I have said, sprang out of the muddled thought of the French Revolution, was then exploited by

Napoleon in his selfish ambition, and subsequently turned to serve the interests of Prussian militarism. After undermining the eighteenth-century "age of reason," it had paved the way for the reign of unreason in the modern age.

Conscription serves to precipitate war, but not to accelerate it —except in the negative sense of accelerating the growth of war-weariness and other underlying causes of defeat. Conscription precipitated war in 1914, owing to the way that the mobilisation of conscript armies disrupted national life and produced an atmosphere in which negotiation became impossible, confirming the warning "mobilisation means war." During that war its effect can be traced in the symptoms which preceded the collapse of the Russian, Austrian, and German armies, as well as the decline of the French and Italian armies. It was the least free states which collapsed under the strain of war, and they collapsed in the order of their degree of unfreedom. By contrast, the best fighting force in the fourth year of war was, by general recognition, the Australian Corps, the force which had rejected conscription and in which there was the least insistence on unthinking obedience.

Significantly, the advocacy of conscription in Britain can be traced back to the years immediately before the war and even prior to the adoption of military conscription, to a time when an influential section of people were more impressed by the social developments of the Nazi system than alarmed by its dangers. A campaign for "universal national service" was launched in the winter before Munich. As defined by Lord Lothian, in a letter to The Times in March 1938, it embodied the "allocation of every individual" to a particular form of service "whether in peace or in emergency." It is being freshly urged now as an "educational" measure.

Such a system entails the suppression of individual judgment. It violates the cardinal principle of a free community: that there should be no restriction of individual freedom save where this is used for active interference with others' freedom. Our tradition of individual freedom is the slow-ripening fruit of centuries of effort. To surrender it within after fighting to defend it against dangers without would be a supremely ironical turn of our history. In respect of personal service, freedom means the right to be true to your convictions, to choose your course, and decide whether the cause is worth service and sacrifice. That is the difference between the free man and the state slave.

Unless the great majority of a people are willing to give their services there is something radically at fault in the state itself. In that case the state is not likely or worthy to survive under test and compulsion will make no serious difference. We may be far from having attained an adequate state of freedom as yet, of economic freedom in particular, but the best assurance of our future lies in advancing conditions in which freedom can live and grow, not in abandoning such essentials of freedom as we have already attained.

In upholding the idea of compulsory service, its advocates have often emphasised that the principle was adopted in our statute law in certain times of alarm and applied in a haphazard way to the poorer classes of the community during the eighteenth and the early nineteenth century. Here they fail to take due account of the progressive development in our national principles and of the way our concept of freedom has been enlarged during the last century.

It was an advance in British civilization which brought us first to question and then to discard the press gang as well as the slave trade. The logical connection between the two institutions, as violations of our principles, was obvious. Is the tide of our civilization now on the ebb?

Another false argument is that since conscription has long been the rule in the Continental countries, including those which remain democracies, we need not fear the effect of adopting it. But the deeper I have gone into the study of war and the history of the past century the further I have come toward the conclusion that the development of conscription has damaged the growth of the idea of freedom in the Continental countries and thereby damaged their efficiency also, by undermining the sense of personal responsibility. There is only too much evidence that the temporary adoption of conscription by England had a permanent effect harmful to the development of freedom and democracy. For my own part, I have come to my present conviction of the supreme importance of freedom through the pursuit of efficiency. I believe that freedom is the foundation of efficiency, both national and military. Thus it is a practical folly as well as a spiritual surrender to "go totalitarian" as a result of fighting for existence against the totalitarian states. Cut off the incentive to freely given service and you dry up the life source of a free community.

We ought to realize that it is easier to adopt the compulsory principle of national life than to shake it off.

Once compulsion for personal service is adopted in peacetime it will be hard to resist the extension of the principle to all other aspects of the nation's life, including freedom of thought, speech, and writing. We ought to think carefully, and to think ahead, before taking a decisive step toward totalitarianism. Or are we so accustomed to our chains that we are no longer conscious of them?

PROGRESS BY COMPULSION?

It is only just to recognize that many of those who advocate such compulsory service are inspired by the desire that it should, and belief that it will, be a means to a good end. This view is one aspect of the larger idea that it is possible to make men good; that they must not only be shown the way to become better but compelled to follow it. That idea has been held by many reformers, most revolutionaries, and all busy-bodies. It has persisted in generation after generation, although as repeatedly contradicted by the experience of history. It is closely related, cousin at least, to the dominant conception of the Communist and Fascist movements.

While pointing out the analogy, and the fallacy, we should draw a distinction, however, between the positive and negative sides of the principle. The negative side comprises all laws which are framed to remove hindrances to progress and prevent interference by a selfish or naturally obstructive section of the community. It may be defined as a process of regulation, as contrasted with actual compulsion, which is, strictly, the positive process of forcing people to do some action against their will. Regulation, in the negative or protective sense of this definition, may be both necessary and helpful in promoting true progress. It does not infringe the principle of freedom, provided that it is wisely applied, for it is embraced in the corollary that freedom does not give license for interference with others' freedom. Moreover, it accords with the philosophical law of progress that the negative paves the way for the positive; that the best chance of ensuring a real step forward lies in taking care to avoid the mistakes that, in experience, have wrecked or distorted past attempts at progress.

At the same time history warns us that even in the negative regulatory sense, if much more in the positive compulsory sense, the effort to achieve progress by decree is apt to lead to reaction. The more hurried the effort, the greater the risk to its endurance. The surer way of achieving progress is by generating and diffusing the thought of improvement. Reforms that last are those that come naturally, and with less friction, when men's minds have become ripe for them. A life spent in sowing a few grains of fruitful thought is a life spent more effectively than in hasty action that produces a crop of weeds. That leads us to see the difference, truly a vital difference, between influence and power.

III. WAR AND PEACE

THE DESIRE FOR POWER

History shows that a main hindrance to real progress is the ever-popular myth of the "great man." While "greatness" may perhaps be used in a comparative sense, if even then referring more to particular qualities than to the embodied sum, the "great man" is a clay idol whose pedestal has been built up by the natural human desire to look up to someone, but whose form has been carved by men who have not yet outgrown the desire to be regarded, or to picture themselves, as great men. Many of those who gain power under present systems have much that is good in them. Few are without some good in them. But to keep their power it is easier, and seems safer, to appeal to the lowest common denominator of the people, to instinct rather than to reason, to interest rather than to right, to expediency rather than to principle. It sounds practical and may thus command respect where to speak of ideals might only arouse distrust. But in practice there is nothing more difficult than to discover where expediency lies, it is apt to lead from one expedient to another, in a vicious circle through endless knots.

THE SHORTSIGHTEDNESS OF EXPEDIENCY

We learn from history that expediency has rarely proved expedient. Yet today perhaps more than ever the statesmen of all countries talk the language of expediency, almost as if they are afraid to label themselves "unpractical" by referring to principles. They are especially fond of emphasising the need for "realism." This attitude would be sound if it implied a sense of the lessons really taught by history. It is unrealistic, for example, to underrate the force of idealism. It is unrealistic, also, to ignore military principles and conditions in taking political steps or making promises. And realism should be combined with foresight, to see one or two moves ahead.

The strength of British policy has been its adaptability to circumstances as they arise; its weakness, that the circumstances (which are usually difficulties) could have been forestalled through forethought. A reflection suggested by the last hundred years of history, especially the history of our affairs in the Mediterranean, is that British policy has been best, not only in spirit but in effect, when it has come nearest to being honest. The counter force of Britain's moral impulses and material interests produced an amazing series of somersaults in British relations with Turkey. We repeatedly sought to cultivate the Sultan as a counterpoise to French or Russian ambitions in the Near East and as often were driven to take action against him because his behaviour to his subjects shocked our sense of justice as well as our sentiments.

In the light of those hundred years of history and their sequel, the use of our national gift for compromise may not seem altogether happy. Such delicate adjustment, to be truly effective, requires a Machiavelli, and the Englishman is not Machiavellian. He can never rid himself of moral scruples sufficiently to fill the part. Thus he is always and inevitably handicapped in an amoral competition, whether in duplicity or blood and iron. Realisation of this inherent "weakness" suggests that Britain might find it better to be more consistently moral. At any rate the experiment has yet to be tried.

On the other hand, there is plenty of experience to show the dilemmas and dangers into which Britain's maladjustment of morality and materialism has landed her. While we complacently counted on the Turks' gratitude, they did not forget the unreliability of our attitude. And by throwing the weight of our influence on the side of the Sultan and his effete palace clique against the movement of the young Turks toward reform, we not only forfeited our influence in restraining their excesses, but cold-shouldered them into the embrace of Germany.

How differently the affairs of the world would go, with a little more decency, a little more honesty, a little more thought! Thought-attempting, above all, to see a few moves ahead and realize the dangers of condoning evil. We try to play the old diplomatic game, yet cannot hope to play it successfully, because we have acquired scruples from which the old-style exponent of realpolitik is free, not yet having grown up as far.

One can understand the point of view of the man who goes in for unabashed "piracy" and seeks his own profit regardless of others. He may draw his profit, although unconsciously his loss far exceeds it, because he is deadening his own soul. But one cannot see sense, even of so shortsighted a kind, in those who maintain any standards of decency in private life yet advocate, or at least countenance, the law of the jungle in public and international affairs. More illogical still are those who talk of patriotic self-sacrifice and of its spiritual sublimity while preaching pure selfishness in world affairs.

What is the use of anyone sacrificing himself to preserve the country unless in the hope, and with the idea, of providing a chance to continue its spiritual progress toward becoming a better country? Otherwise he is merely helping to preserve the husk, saving the form but not the soul. Only a perverse patriotism is capable of such hopeless folly.

What is the value of patriotism if it means no more than a cat's devotion to its own fireside rather than to human beings? And, like the cat, such a "patriot" is apt to get burned when the house catches fire.

THE IMPORTANCE OF KEEPING PROMISES

Civilization is built on the practice of keeping promises. It may not sound a high attainment, but if trust in its observance be shaken the whole structure cracks and sinks. Any constructive effort and all human relations, personal, political, and commercial, depend on being able to depend on promises.

This truth has a reflection on the question of collective security among nations and on the lessons of history in regard to that subject. In the years before the war the charge was constantly brought that its supporters were courting the risk of war by their exaggerated respect for covenants. Although they may have been fools in disregarding the conditions necessary for the effective fulfilment of pledges, they at least showed themselves men of honour and, in a long view, of more fundamental common sense than those who argued that we should give aggressors a free hand so long as they left us alone.

History has shown, repeatedly, that the hope of buying safety in this way is the greatest of delusions.

THE IMPORTANCE OF CARE ABOUT MAKING PROMISES

It is immoral to make promises that one cannot in practice fulfil in the sense that the recipient expects. On that ground, in 1939 I questioned the underlying morality of the Polish Guarantee, as well as its practicality. If the Poles had realized the military inability of Britain and France to save them from defeat, and of what such defeat would mean to them individually and collectively, it is unlikely that they would have shown such stubborn opposition to Germany's originally modest demands for Danzig and a passage through the Corridor. Since it was obvious to me that they were bound to lose these points, and much more in the event of a conflict, it seemed to me wrong on our part to make promises that were bound to encourage false hopes.

It also seemed to me that any such promises were the most certain way to produce war, because of the inevitable provocativeness of guaranteeing, at such a moment of tension, an area which we had hitherto treated as outside our sphere of interest; because of the manifest temptation which the guarantee offered, to a military-minded people like the Germans, to show how fatuously impractical our guarantee was; and because of its natural effect in stiffening the attitude of a people, the Poles, who had always shown themselves exceptionally intractable in negotiating a reasonable settlement of any issue.

An historian could not help seeing certain parallels between the long-standing aspect of the Polish-German situation and that between Britain and the Boer Republics forty years earlier, and remembering the effect on us of the attempts of the other European powers to induce or coerce us into negotiating a settlement with the Boers. If our own reaction then had been so violent, it could hardly be expected that the reaction of a nation filled with an even more bellicose spirit would be less violent, especially as the attempt to compel negotiation was backed by an actual promise of making war if Poland felt moved to resist the German conditions.

It is worth recalling that Gladstone, than whom no one was more emphatic in condemning aggression, defined, for Queen Victoria's enlightenment, a series of guiding principles for British foreign policy when he first became Prime Minister in 1869. The circumstances then, before collective security had been organized, were broadly similar to those of 1939, when it had been in effect dissolved.

Among the introductory remarks, which are still relevant and not only, nor now primarily, to England, he said: "Though Europe never saw England faint away, we know at what cost of internal danger to all the institutions of the country she fought her way to the perilous eminence on which she undoubtedly stood in 1815. ... Is England so uplifted in strength above every other nation that she can with prudence advertise herself as ready to undertake the general redress of wrongs? Would not the consequences of such professions and promises be either the premature exhaustion of her means, or a collapse in the day of performance?"

The principles he laid down were "That England should keep entire in her own hands the means of estimating her own obligations; . . . that she should not narrow her own liberty of choice by declarations made to other Powers ... of which they would claim to be at least joint interpreters; . . . that, come what may, it is better for her to promise too little than too much; that she should not encourage the weak by giving expectations of aid to resist the strong, but should rather seek to deter the strong by firm but moderate language, from aggressions on the weak."

THE GERMS OF WAR

Such pitfalls of policy are closely related to the causes of war itself. Sympathies and antipathies, interests and loyalties, cloud the vision. And this kind of short-sight is apt to produce short temper.

As a light on the processes by which wars are manufactured and detonated, there is nothing more illuminating than a study of the fifty years of history preceding 1914. The vital influences are to be detected not in the formal documents compiled by rulers, ministers, and generals but in their marginal notes and verbal asides. Here are revealed their instinctive prejudices, lack of interest in truth for its own sake, and indifference to the exactness of statement and reception which is a safeguard against dangerous misunderstanding.

I have come to think that accuracy, in the deepest sense, is the basic virtue, the foundation of understanding, supporting the promise of progress. The cause of most troubles can be traced to excess; the failure to check them to deficiency; their prevention lies in moderation. So in the case of troubles that develop from spoken or written communication, their cause can be traced to overstatement, their maintenance to understatement, while their prevention lies in exact statement. It applies to private as well as to public life.

Sweeping judgments, malicious gossip, inaccurate statements which spread a misleading impression; these are symptoms of the moral and mental recklessness that gives rise to war. Studying their effect, one is led to see that the germs of war lie within ourselves, not in economics, politics, or religion as such. How can we hope to rid the world of war until we have cured ourselves of the originating causes?

HOW THE GERMS WORK

These germs are most virulent among those who direct the affairs of nations. The atmosphere of power, and activity in the pursuit of power, inflame them. The way they work can be clearly traced in examining the origins and course of World War I. While economic factors formed a predisposing cause, the deeper and more decisive factors lay in human nature, its possessiveness, competitiveness, vanity, and pugnacity, all of which were fomented by the dishonesty which breeds inaccuracy.

Throughout the twenty-five years preceding that war, one of the most significant symptoms can be seen in the Kaiser's vanity and the effect on it of his curiously mingled affection and jealousy toward England. Understanding of his composition enables us to see how his worst tendencies were often sharpened by the snubs that Edward VII was disposed to administer to his nephew.

When one comes to the fateful weeks preceding the outbreak of war, one sees how great was the part played in the Governments of both Austria and Russia by resentment at past humiliations and the fear of any fresh "loss of face." Both of those Governments, and their foreign ministers in particular, were all too ready to bring misery upon millions rather than swallow their injured pride. And in the crucial opening phase of the crisis, the Austrian Government was prompted to take up a position from which it could not easily climb down, by the encouragement which the Kaiser gave it to take vigorous action.

The irony of history, and the absurdity of the factors that determine it, was never more clearly shown than at that moment. The crisis arose out of the murder of the Archduke Franz Ferdinand of Austria by a handful of young Slavs who had sought and received help from a Serbian secret society known as the "Black Hand." They murdered the one man of influence in Austria who was potentially their friend and might have fulfilled their hopes.

The Austrian Government, while quite pleased at his removal, used it as an excuse for curbing Serbia. The Kaiser's initial support of their high-handed treatment of Serbia seems to have been inspired by his royal indignation that royal blood should have been shed, together with his fear that if he advised moderation he would be reproached with weakness. When he saw war actually in sight he tried to back down, but it was then too late. And the Austrian Government, in turn, was afraid that if it showed hesitation it might subsequently forfeit Germany's support. So it hastily declared war on Serbia, regardless of the risks of bringing on a general war.

The threat to Serbia was an affront to Russia, whose Government regarded that Slav country as its protege. Having already been assured of France's support, the Russian Government now decided to mobilise its forces on the Austrian frontier. But the military then intervened with the argument that it was technically impracticable to carry out such a partial mobilisation, and they insisted on a general mobilisation embracing the German frontier also.

The military, with their "military reasons," now to all intents took charge everywhere. The German General Staff, which had been privately inciting the Austrian General Staff to exploit the situation, was now able to use the Russian mobilisation as a means to overcome the Kaiser's belated caution. Arguing that the military situation was more favourable than it might be later, they succeeded in securing a declaration of war against Russia. That in turn involved war with France, not merely because France was Russia's ally but because the German military plan had been framed to meet the case of war with both countries simultaneously and was so inflexible in design that it could not be modified without disrupting it. So, despite the feeble protests of the Kaiser and his chancellor, war was declared on France as well as on Russia.

As the long-standing German military plan had been designed to circumvent the French frontier fortresses by going through Belgium, the violation of her neutrality involved Britain, as one of its guarantors, cutting the "Gordian knot" of the triangle into which we had got by exchanging our traditional policy of isolation for a semi-detached arrangement with France that was, in turn, complicated by the way the General Staff had made detailed transport arrangements with the French General Staff behind the Cabinet's back.

The war we were drawn stumblingly into was, on our side, a striking example of the drawbacks of entering into vague commitments without thinking out the implications and the military problems. It was, on the other side, a glaring example of the folly of allowing the purely military mind to frame hard-and-fast plans, on technical grounds, without regard to wiser considerations, political, economic and moral. As a result, when the original military plan went wrong, Germany found herself in a hole from which she could not extricate herself.

HOW THE GERMS PERSIST

Similar influences wrecked every good chance of bringing the war to an end, on satisfactory terms, before all the countries were exhausted. In 1917, the peace party in Germany gained an ascendancy over the Kaiser and were prepared not only to withdraw from all the conquered territory but actually to cede all but a fraction of Alsace-Lorraine to France, in other words, to give her as much as she actually gained in the end without further sacrifice of life.

As was later disclosed by Lord Esher, the prospect was frustrated, and the British Government kept in the dark about it, by M. Ribot's petty-minded resentment that the approach had been made through M. Briand. "The underlying motive was jealousy on the part of the [French] Foreign Minister and Foreign Office." When the facts subsequently became known, they caused the fall of M. Ribot. But by that time the Kaiser had been thrown back into the arms of the war party by the repulse of the offer.

Similarly, when the new Emperor of Austria tried to break away from Germany and make peace, his advance was rebuffed and a splendid opportunity lost, because it ran contrary to the inordinate ambitions of Signor Sonnino, the Italian Foreign Minister, and those of M. Poincare in France. The overture was hidden both from our Government and the American and was skilfully wrecked by the mean expedient of letting the Germans know what the Austrian Emperor was proposing, thus giving him away to his unwanted partner.

On that side, the personal wrangles and wire-pulling were just as common and constant. Nothing more illuminating has been written than the reflection to which General Hoffmann, perhaps the ablest brain in the German High Command, was brought by his experience of watching the tug of war between the Falkenhayn faction and the Hindenburg-Ludendorff faction. His reflection is worth quoting:

When one gets a close view of influential people, their bad relations with each other, their conflicting ambitions, all the slander and the hatred, one must always bear in mind that it is certainly much worse on the other side, among the French, English, and Russians, or one might well be nervous. . . . The race for power and personal positions seems to destroy all men's characters. I believe that the only creature who can keep his honour is a man living on his own estate; he has no need to intrigue and struggle, for it is no good intriguing for fine weather.

Any history of war which treats only of its strategic and political course is merely a picture of the surface. The personal currents run deeper and may have a deeper influence on the outcome. Well might Hoffmann remark: "For the first time in my life I have seen 'History' at close quarters, and I now know that its actual process is very different to what is presented to posterity."

We learn from history that war breeds war. That is natural. The atmosphere of war stimulates all varieties of the bellicose bacilli, and these lend to find favourable conditions in the aftermath in what, with unconscious irony, is usually described as the restoration of peace.

Conditions are especially favourable to their renewal in the aftermath of a long and exhausting war and most of all in a war which ends with the appearance of a definite victory for one of the belligerent sides. For then, those who belong to the defeated side naturally tend to put the blame for all their troubles upon the victors and thus upon the simple fact of defeat instead of upon their own folly. They feel that if they had won they would have avoided any ill-effects.

THE ILLUSION OF VICTORY

We learn from history that complete victory has never been completed by the result that the victors always anticipate: a good and lasting peace. For victory has always sown the seeds of a fresh war, because victory breeds among the vanquished a desire for vindication and vengeance and because victory raises fresh rivals. In the case of a victory gained by an alliance, the most common case, this is a most common sequel. It seems to be the natural result of the removal of a strong third-party check.

The first lesson has always been recognized when passions cool. The second is not so obvious, so that it may be worth amplification. A too complete victory inevitably complicates the problem of making a just and wise peace settlement. Where there is no longer the counterbalance of an opposing force to control the appetites of the victors, there is no check on the conflict of views and interests between the parties to the alliance. The divergence is then apt to become so acute as to turn the comradeship of common danger into the hospitality of mutual dissatisfaction so that the ally of one war becomes the enemy in the next.

Victory in the true sense implies that the state of peace, and of one's people, is better after the war than before. Victory in this sense is only possible if a quick result can be gained or if a long effort can be economically proportioned to the national resources. The end must be adjusted to the means. It is wiser to run risks of-war for the sake of preserving peace than to run risks of exhaustion in war for the sake of finishing with victory, a conclusion that runs counter to custom but is supported by experience. Indeed, deepening study of past experience leads to the conclusion that nations might often have come nearer to their object by taking advantage of a lull in the struggle to discuss a settlement than by pursuing the war with the aim of "victory."

Where the two sides are too evenly matched to offer a reasonable chance of early success to either, the statesman is wise who can learn something from the psychology of strategy. It is an elementary principle of strategy that, if you find your opponent in a strong position costly to force, you should leave him a line of retreat as the quickest way of loosening his resistance. It should, equally, be a principle of policy, especially in war, to provide your opponent with a ladder by which he can climb down.

THE IMPORTANCE OF MODERATION

We learn from history that after any long war the survivors are apt to reach common agreement that there has been no real victor but only common losers. War is only profitable if victory is quickly gained. Only an aggressor can hope to gain a quick victory. If he is frustrated, the war is bound to be long, and mutually ruinous, unless it is brought to an end by mutual agreement.

Since an aggressor goes to war for gain, he is apt to be the more ready of the two sides to seek peace by agreement. The aggressed side is usually more inclined to seek vengeance through the pursuit of victory; even though all experience has shown that victory is a mirage in the desert created by a long war. This desire for vengeance is natural but far reaching and self-injurious. And even if it be fulfilled, it merely sets up a fresh cycle of revenge-seeking. Hence any wise statesman should be disposed to consider the possibility of ending the war by agreement as soon as it is clear that the war will otherwise be a prolonged one.

The side that has suffered aggression would be unwise to bid for peace lest its bid be taken as a sign of weakness or fear. But it would be wise to listen to any bid that the enemy makes. Even if the initial proposals are not good enough, once an opposing Government has started bidding it is easily led to improve its offers. And this is the best way to loosen its hold on its troops and people, who naturally tend to desire peace, so long as they can regain it without being conquered, when they find that the prospect of a cheap victory is fading. By contrast, the will to fight always tends to become stronger among the people who have been attacked, so that it is easier to make them hold out in any negotiation for terms that are satisfying.

The history of ancient Greece showed that, in a democracy, emotion dominates reason to a greater extent than in any other political system, thus giving freer rein to the passions which sweep a state into war and prevent it getting out at any point short of the exhaustion and destruction of one or other of the opposing sides. Democracy is a system which puts a break on preparation for war, aggressive or defensive, but it is not one that conduces to the limitation of warfare or the prospects of a good peace. No political system more easily becomes out of control when passions are aroused. These defects have been multiplied in modern democracies, since their great extension of size and their vast electorate produce a much larger volume of emotional pressure.

History should have taught the statesman that there is no practical halfway house between a peace of complete subjugation and a peace of true moderation. History also shows that the former is apt to involve the victor in endless difficulties, unless it is carried so far as to amount to extermination, which is not practicable. The latter requires a settlement so reasonable that the losers will not only accept it but see the advantages of maintaining it in their own interests.

Wellington's best contribution to the future of Europe, after victory was gained, was in the making of the peace settlement with France. In the occupation of the conquered country he was as intent to protect the people from ill-usage as he had been when that policy had been a means to smooth the path of his invasion. He did all he could to curb the revengeful excesses of his allies, even to the point of posting a British sentry on the Pont de Jena in Paris to hinder Blücher from blowing it up, while insisting that his own army must set an example of gentleness, courtesy, and restraint.

When it came to drawing up the peace terms, he threw all his influence against the demand of Prussia and the other German states that France should be dismembered and compelled to pay a huge indemnity, to compensate their sufferings and safeguard their security. He realized with uncommon clarity the unwisdom of immoderation and the fundamental insecurity of a peace based upon oppression. The outcome justified his policy of moderation.

It was because he really understood war that he became so good at securing peace. He was the least militaristic of soldiers and free from the lust of glory. It was because he saw the value of peace that he became so unbeatable in war. For he kept the end in view, instead of falling in love with the means. Unlike Napoleon, he was not infected by the romance of war, which generates illusions and self-deceptions. That was how Napoleon had failed and Wellington prevailed.

It is a recurrent illusion in history that the enemy of the time is essentially different, in the sense of being more evil, than any in the past. It is remarkable to see how not only the impression but the phrases repeat themselves. And even historians are apt to lose their balance when they turn from the past to the problems of their own time. The eminent historian Stubbs, writing in 1860, when Britain feared an invasion by Napoleon III, asked why "the English and the Germans have always been the peace-loving nations of history" (an extremely unhistorical remark in both cases). He answered his own question: "Because France shows herself today as she has been throughout the course of a thousand years, aggressive, unscrupulous, false."

There is a widespread feeling in the West that no "coexistence" compromise is really possible, or likely to last, with the Communist regimes of Russia and China, and that these will continue to exploit opportunities and grab more gains wherever they can. That feeling has much justification in experience and in knowledge of totalitarian trends. But the more right it is, the more vital that Western statesmen in taking countermeasures should bear in mind a long-standing lesson of police experience that "a burglar doesn't commit murder unless he is cornered." It is as true of the community of nations as of any smaller one.

On the other hand, tension is almost bound to relax eventually if war is postponed long enough. This has happened often before in history, for situations change. They never remain static. But it is always dangerous to be too dynamic, and impatient, in trying to force the pace. A war-charged situation can only change two ways. It is bound to become better, eventually, if war is avoided without surrender.

THE ILLUSION OF TREATIES

One of the clear lessons that history teaches is that no agreement between Governments has had any stability beyond their recognition that it is in their own interests to continue to adhere to it. I cannot conceive that any serious student of history would be impressed by such a hollow phrase as "the sanctity of treaties."

We must face the fact that international relations are governed by interests and not by moral principles. Then it can be seen that the validity of treaties depends on mutual convenience. This can provide an effective guarantee. While there is no security in negotiating from weakness, there is a better prospect in any negotiation where it is clear that the strength of both sides is closely balanced. For in that case any settlement is based on a mutual recognition that the prospects of a one-sided victory would be incommensurate with the prospects of mutual exhaustion and of the consequent subjection of both parties subsequently to the interests of third parties who are standing outside the struggle or participating to only a limited extent.

The Romans coined the maxim "If you wish for peace, prepare for war." But the many wars they fought, and the endless series since their day, show that there was a fallacy in the argument or that it was too simply put, without sufficient thought. As Calvin Coolidge caustically remarked after World War I: "No nation ever had an army large enough to guarantee it against attack in time of peace, or ensure it victory in time of war."

In studying how wars have broken out I was led to suggest, after World War I, that a truer maxim would be "If you wish for peace, understand war." That conclusion was reinforced by World War II and its sequel. It signposts a road to peace that is more hopeful than building plans which have so often proved "castles in the air."

Any plan for peace is apt to be not only futile but dangerous. Like most planning, unless of a mainly material kind, it breaks down through disregard of human nature. Worse still, the higher the hopes that are built on such a plan, the more likely that their collapse may precipitate war.

There is no panacea for peace that can be written out in a formula like a doctor's prescription. But one can set down a series of practical points; elementary principles drawn from the sum of human experience in all times. Study war and learn from its history. Keep strong, if possible. In any case, keep cool. Have unlimited patience. Never corner an opponent and always assist him to save his face. Put yourself in his shoes so as to see things through his eyes. Avoid self-righteousness like the devil; nothing is so self-blinding. Cure yourself of two commonly fatal delusions: the idea of victory and the idea that war cannot be limited.

These points were all made, explicitly or implicitly, in the earliest known book on the problems of war and peace, Sun Tzu's, about 500 B.C. The many wars, mostly futile, that have occurred since then show how little the nations have learned from history. But the lesson has been more deeply engraved. And now, since the development of the H-bomb, the only hope of survival, for either side, rests on careful maintenance of these eight pillars of policy.

THE DILEMMA OF THE INTELLECTUAL

Neither intellectuals nor their critics appear to recognize the inherent dilemma of the thinking man and

its inevitability. The dilemma should be faced, for it is a
natural part of the growth of any human mind.

An intellectual ought to realize the extent to which the
world is shaped by human emotions, emotions
uncontrolled by reason; his thinking must have been
shallow, and his observation narrow, if he fails to realize
that. Having once learned to think and to use reason as a
guide, however, he cannot possibly float with the current
of popular emotion and fluctuate with its violent changes
unless he himself ceases to think or is deliberately false to
his own thought. And in the latter case it is likely that he
will commit intellectual suicide, gradually, "by the death
of a thousand cuts."

A deeper diagnosis of the malady from which left-wing
intellectuals have suffered in the past might suggest that
their troubles have come not from following reason too far
but from not following it far enough to realize the general
power of unreason. Many of them also seem to have
suffered from failing to apply reason internally as well as
externally through not using it for the control of their own
emotions. In that way, they unwittingly helped to get this
country into the mess of the last war and then found
themselves in an intellectual mess as a result.

In one of the more penetrating criticisms written on this
subject, George Orwell expressed a profound truth in
saying that "the energy that actually shapes the world
springs from emotions." He referred to the deep-seated
and dynamic power of "racial pride, leader-worship,
religious belief, love of war." There are powerful emotions
beyond these, however. The energy of the intellectual
himself springs from an emotion: love of truth, the desire

for wider knowledge and understanding. That emotion has done quite a lot to shape the world, as a study of world history amply shows. In the thinking man that source of energy dries up only when he ceases to believe in the guiding power of thought and allows himself to become merely a vehicle for the prevailing popular emotions of the moment.

Bertrand Russell remarked in 1964 that the "task of persuading governments and populations of the disasters of nuclear war had been very largely accomplished" and went on to say that it had been "accomplished by a combination of methods of agitation." If there is one thing that seems to be clear, it is that such methods have had very little effect compared with the effect of logical argument in converting the mind of the military leadership to a realisation that nuclear war is futile and suicidal.

History bears witness to the vital part that the "prophets" have played in human progress, which is evidence of the ultimate practical value of expressing unreservedly the truth as one sees it. Yet it also becomes clear that the acceptance and spreading of their vision has always depended on another class of men, "leaders" who had to be philosophical strategists, striking a compromise between truth and men's receptivity to it. Their effect has often depended as much on their own limitations in perceiving the truth as on their practical wisdom in proclaiming it.

The prophets must be stoned; that is their lot and the test of their self fulfilment. A leader who is stoned, however, may merely prove that he has failed in his function through a deficiency of wisdom or through confusing his function with that of a prophet. Time alone can tell whether the effect of such a sacrifice redeems the apparent failure as a leader that does honour to him as a man. At the least, he avoids the more common fault of leaders, that of sacrificing the truth to expediency without ultimate advantage to the cause. For whoever habitually suppresses the truth in the interests of tact will produce a deformity from the womb of his thought.

Is there a practical way of combining progress toward the attainment of truth with progress toward its acceptance? A possible solution of the problem is suggested by reflection on strategic principles which point to the importance of maintaining an object consistently and, also, of pursuing it in a way adapted to circumstances.

Opposition to the truth is inevitable, especially if it takes the form of a new idea, but the degree of resistance can be diminished by giving thought not only to the aim but to the method of approach. Avoid a frontal attack on a long-established position; instead, seek to turn it by a flank movement, so that a more penetrable side is exposed to the thrust of truth. But in any such indirect approach, take care not to diverge from the truth, for nothing is more fatal to its real advancement than to lapse into untruth.

The meaning of these reflections may be made clearer by illustration from one's own experience. Looking back on the stages by which various fresh ideas gained acceptance, it can be seen that the process was eased when they could be presented not as something radically new but as the revival in modern terms of a time-honoured principle or practice that had been forgotten. This required not deception but care to trace the connection since "there is nothing new under the sun."

A notable example was the way that the opposition to mechanisation was diminished by showing that the mobile armoured vehicle, the fast-moving tank, was fundamentally the heir of the armoured horseman and thus the natural means-of reviving the decisive role which cavalry had played in past ages.

THE LIMITATIONS OF CONFORMITY

Even among great scholars there is no more unhistorical fallacy than that, in order to command, you must learn to obey. A more temperamentally insubordinate lot than the outstanding soldiers and sailors of the past could scarcely be found in England one has only to think of Wolfe and Wellington, Nelson and Dundonald; in France, Napoleon's marshals in this respect at least were worthy of their master.

Robert E. Lee's conduct at West Point was so immaculate that he had not a single offence recorded against him, while he became known among his fellows as the "Marble Model." What a contrast this offers to the experience of Sherman and Grant, who were both often unbearably irked by the petty restrictions and often kicked over the traces. For Sherman, even when looking back upon it when he had risen to be commanding general of the United States Army, sarcastically wrote: "Then, as now, neatness in dress and form, with a strict conformity to the rules, were the qualifications for office, and I suppose I was not found to excel in any of these." As for Grant, when a cadet he fervently prayed for the success of a bill to abolish the institution so that he might be released from its constant vexations!

Comparing their youthful record with Lee's, any student of psychology would be inclined to predict that they had more promise of being successful commanders in later life if given the chance. Also that, if either were to be pitted against him in war's grim test, they were more likely to come out on top.

A model boy rarely goes far, and even when he does he is apt to falter when severely tested. A boy who conforms immaculately to school rules is not likely to grow into a man who will conquer by breaking the stereotyped professional rules of his time, as conquest has most often been achieved. Still less does it imply the development of the wide views necessary in a man who is not merely a troop commander but the strategic adviser of his Government. The wonderful thing about Lee's generalship is not his legendary genius but the way he rose above his handicaps, handicaps that were internal even more than external.

THE PROBLEM OF FORCE

The more I have reflected on the experience of history the more I have come to see the instability of solutions achieved by force and to suspect even those instances where force has had the appearance of resolving difficulties. But the question remains whether we can afford to eliminate force in the world as it is without risking the loss of such ground as reason has gained.

Beyond this is the doubt whether we should be able to eliminate it even if we had the strength of mind to take such a risk. For weaker minds will cling to this protection and by so doing spoil the possible effectiveness of non-resistance. Is there any way out of the dilemma?

There is at least one solution that has yet to be tried; that the masters of force should be those who have mastered all desire to employ it. That solution is an extension of what Bernard Shaw expressed in Major Barbara: that wars would continue until the makers of gunpowder became professors of Greek, and he here had Gilbert Murray in mind, or the professors of Greek became the makers of gunpowder. And this, in turn, was derived from Plato's conclusion that the affairs of mankind would never go right until either the rulers became philosophers or the philosophers became the rulers.

If armed forces were controlled by men who have become convinced of the wrongness of using force there would be the nearest approach to a safe assurance against its abuse. Such men might also come closest to efficiency in its use, should the enemies of civilization compel this. For the more complex that war becomes the more its efficient direction depends on understanding its properties and effects; and the deeper the study of modern war is carried the stronger grows the conviction of its futility.

THE PROBLEM OF LIMITING WAR

Can war be limited? Logic says, "No. War is the sphere of violence, and it would be illogical to hesitate in using any extreme of violence that can help you to win the war."

History replies, "Such logic makes nonsense. You go to war to win the peace, not just for the sake of fighting. Extremes of violence may frustrate your purpose, so that victory becomes a boomerang. Moreover, it is a matter of historical fact that war has been limited in many ways."

Read Julius Caesar's own account of his campaigns in Gaul, and you may realize that Hitler was quite a gentle man compared with that much praised missionary of Roman civilization who is revered by so many students of the classic. But the Romans at their worst were mild compared with our own ancestors, and the ancestors of all the Western European nations, during the Dark Ages that followed the collapse of the Roman Empire and the *Pax Romana*. It was the habit of the Saxons and the Franks to slay everyone in their path, men, women, and children and to indulge in the most reckless destruction of towns and crops.

It is important to understand how the "total warfare" of those times came to be modified and gradually humanised. It is a story of "ups and downs," but far more up than down.

The first influence in the rescue of humanity was the Christian Church. Even before it converted the pagan conquerors of the West, it often succeeded in restraining their savagery by exploiting their superstitions. One of its most notable efforts was the two-branched "truce of God." The *Pax Dei* introduced in the tenth century sought to insure immunity for non-combatants and their property. It was followed by the *Treuga Dei*, which sought to limit the number of days on which fighting could take place by establishing periods of truce.

A wider reinforcement came from the Code of Chivalry. This seems to have been of Arabic origin. Here it has to be admitted that the followers of Mohammed were much quicker than the followers of Christ, in the West, to develop humane habits although Mohammed himself had shown much more of the *Old Testament* spirit revealed in Moses. Contact with the East, however, helped to foster the growth of chivalry in the West. That code, for all its faults, helped to humanise warfare by formalising it.

Economic factors also helped. The custom of releasing prisoners in exchange for a ransom may have depended more on a profit motive than on a sense of chivalrous behaviour, but was essentially good sense; it worked for good. At first it applied only to those who could afford to pay a ransom. But the habit grew, as habits do, and gave rise to a general custom of sparing the lives of the defeated. That was an immense step forward.

This increasing habit of limitation was aided by the spread of mercenary soldiers, that is, professional soldiers. First, these came to realize the mutual benefit of restraint in dealing with one another. Then their employers came to realize the mutual benefit of curbing their tendency to plunder the civilian population on either side.

Unhappily, a severe setback came from the Wars of Religion, which arose from the Reformation. Religious fervour incited barbarous behaviour. The split in the Church broke up its moral authority, while turning it from a restraining influence into an impelling agent. It heated the fires of hatred and inflamed the passions of war. The climax of this period was the Thirty Years' War, when more than half the population of the German states perished, directly or indirectly, from the war.

Yet the savagery of such warfare was not so great as it had been in the Dark Ages. Moreover, this excess of violence produced a widespread revulsion, which, in turn, led to a great advance, greater than ever before. To proceed to extremes in war might be logical, but it was not reasonable.

Another important influence was the growth of more formal and courteous manners in social life. This code of manners spread into the field of international relations. These two factors, reason and manners, saved civilization when it was on the verge of collapse. Men came to feel that behaviour mattered more than belief, and customs more than creeds, in making earthly life tolerable and human relations workable.

The improvement made during the eighteenth century in the customs of war, and in reducing its evils, forms one of the great achievements of civilization. It opened up a prospect that the progressive limitation of war, by formalisation, might lead to its elimination. The improvement was helped by the fact that there was no radical change in the means of warfare during this period. For experience suggests that an increase of savagery in warfare is apt to follow new developments, technical or political, which unsettle the existing order.

The bad effect of a big political change was shown at the end of the eighteenth century, when the code of limitations on violence in war was broken down by the French Revolution. But the wars of the French Revolution never, at their worst, became so terrible as the religious wars of the seventeenth century. And the restoration of civilization was helped by the wise moderation of the peace terms imposed on France after the fall of Napoleon, thanks largely to England's influence, as represented by Wellington and Castlereagh. The best testimony to it was that half a century passed before there was another serious war in Europe.

The nineteenth century saw, on the whole, a continuance of the trend toward humane limitations in warfare. This was registered in the Geneva conventions of 1864 and 1906, which dealt mainly with the protection of the wounded, and the Hague conventions of 1899 and 1907, which covered a wider field.

Civil wars have tended toward the worst excesses and the nineteenth century saw a significant extension of such conflicts.

The American Civil War was the first in which the railway, the steamship, and telegraphy were important factors, and these new instruments had revolutionary effects on strategy. Another important change came from the growth of population and the trend toward centralisation, both being the products of a growing industrialisation. The sum effect was to increase the economic target, and also the moral target, while making both more vulnerable. This in turn increased the incentive to strike at the sources of the opponent's armed power instead of striking at its shield, the armed forces.

This was the first war between modern democracies, and Sherman saw very clearly that the resisting power of a democracy depends even more on the strength of the people's will than on the strength of its armies. His strategy was ably fitted to fulfil the primary aim of his grand strategy. His unchecked march through the heart of the South, destroying its resources, was the most effective way to create and spread a sense of helplessness that would undermine the will to continue the war.

The havoc that Sherman's march produced in the opponent's back areas left a legacy of bitterness in later years that has recoiled on Sherman's historical reputation. But it is questionable whether that bitterness or the impoverishment of the South would have been prolonged, or grave, if the peace settlement had not been dominated by the vindictiveness of the Northern extremists who gained the upper hand after Lincoln's assassination. For Sherman himself bore in mind the need of moderation in making peace. That was shown in the generous terms of the agreement he drafted for the surrender of Johnston's army, an offer for which he was violently denounced by the Government in Washington. Moreover, he persistently pressed the importance, for the future of the forcibly reunited nation, of reconciling the conquered section by good treatment and helping its recovery.

The humane progress of war was now to be endangered by three factors. One was the survival of conscription. Another was the growth of a new theory of war which embodied all the most dangerous features of revolutionary and Napoleonic practice. That theory was evolved in Prussia by Clausewitz. Pursuing logic to the extreme, he argued that moderation had no place in war: "War is an act of violence pursued to the utmost." As his thinking proceeded he came to realize the fallacy of such logic. Unfortunately, he died before he could revise his writings and his disciples remembered only his extreme starting point. A further dangerous factor was also developing, the terrific scientific improvement in the weapons of war.

Under the combined influence of these factors the 1914-18 war started in a bad way and went from bad to worse. The ill-effects of the war were deepened by the nature of the peace settlement. Any people whose spirit was not permanently broken would have striven to evade such crippling and humiliating terms. The prospects were made worse by the state of exhaustion and chaos to which Europe was reduced by the time the peace was made and by the general degeneration of standards produced by the years of unlimited violence.

The first effect was seen before World War II began in the more complete organization of the people for the service of the state. The second effect was seen in the more drastic, and often atrocious, treatment of conquered populations during that war.

On the military side, in contrast, the level of behaviour was better in a number of respects than in World War I. Even at its worst it never fell back to the pre-eighteenth century level. The armies in general continued to observe many of the rules contained in the established code of war. Indeed, military atrocities seem to have been fewer than in World War I.

Unfortunately, such a gain for civilization was offset by the development of new weapons for which no clear limitations had been thought out and no code of rules established in time. As a result the immense growth of air power led to a sweeping disregard for humane limitations on its action, in carrying out bombardment from the air. This produced an extent of devastation, and in many areas a degradation of living conditions, worse than anything seen since the Thirty Years' War. Indeed, in the destruction of cities, the record of World War II exceeds anything since the campaigns of Genghis Khan and Tamerlane.

"Total warfare," such as we have known it hitherto, is not compatible with the atomic age. Total warfare implies that the aim, the effort, and the degree of violence are unlimited. An unlimited war waged with atomic power would make worse than nonsense; it would be mutually suicidal. The most likely form of conflict for the next generation is what I call "subversive war." Otherwise it can only be some other form of "limited" warfare.

THE PROBLEM OF DISARMAMENT

"Disarmament" was a late starter in the race, at snail's pace, for international security following World War I. After protracted preliminary discussions the World Disarmament Conference finally assembled at Geneva in 1932. A few months before it opened, Japan had tentatively started on its long course of aggression in the Far East.

In the second year after the end of World War II, there was a revival of the project. Disarmament suddenly came to the fore in the proceedings of the United Nations although there had been no mention of it in the agenda when the General Assembly met in New York in the autumn of 1946.

The revival came in an indirect way, arising out of a Soviet proposal for a census of the troops which each nation was maintaining abroad. This led at first merely to a series of wrangles. But it led on to an unexpected resolution for a general reduction of armaments, and then, surprisingly, to acceptance of international inspection in principle, which had previously been opposed as an infringement of national sovereignty. A partial implementation of this principle was reached in the Kennedy-Khrushchev Test Ban Treaty.

Experience shows that a basic flaw, though not the most obvious one, in any scheme of international security or disarmament has been the difficulty of reconciling the view of the expert advisers. Conferences have repeatedly been spun out by the technical pros and contras, until the prospect of agreement wore thin and the political temper became frayed. That is hardly surprising.

To take the opinion of generals, admirals, or air marshals on the deeper problems of war, as distinct from its executive technique, is like consulting your local pharmacist about the treatment of a deep-seated disease. However skilled in compounding drugs, it is not their concern to study the causes and consequences of the disease, nor the psychology of the sufferers.

While experience has shown the insecurity of international plans for the prevention of war, earlier experience shows that it is possible to develop an international habit of observing limitations, from a shrewd realisation that mutual restraint is beneficial to self-interest in the long run. The more that warfare is "formalised" the less damaging it proves. Past efforts in this direction have had more success than is commonly appreciated.

War between independent states which acknowledge no superior sovereignty has a basic likeness to a fight between individual men. In the process of restricting such murderous fights, the judicial combat of the early Middle Ages served a useful purpose until such time as the authority of the state was wide enough and strong enough to enforce a judgment by law. The formal rules of judicial combat came to be respected long before "individual warfare" was effectively abolished in favour of a judicial decision by legal process. The value of such rules was aptly summed up in Montesquieu's *Esprit des Lois*, where he remarks that, just as many wise things are conducted in a very foolish manner, so some foolish things have been conducted in a very wise manner.

When the authority of Church and State was shaken by the disruptive conflicts of the later Middle Ages, individual warfare was revived in the guise of duelling. In sixteenth-century Italy, its dangers were curbed by such a multiplication of rules that it faded out, formality gradually producing nullity. Elsewhere, especially in France, the duel had a longer run, but it can be seen that its increasing formalisation was an important factor in assisting the efforts of law, reason, and humane feeling to suppress the practice. Even at the worst, the custom of the duel provided a regulated outlet for violent feelings which checked a more rampant revival of individual killing.

In a similar way, the wars between the Italian city-states of the Renaissance period, and the greater ones between the European nation-states of the eighteenth century, not only bore witness to human pugnacity but provided evidence of the possibility of regulating it. They were an outlet for the aggressive instincts and for the types of men who are naturally combative, while keeping their violence within bounds, to the benefit of civilization. Such warfare may have been more of a necessity than idealists would care to recognize, but in limiting the evil they served a better purpose than is generally realized.

THE PROBLEM OF IRREGULAR WARFARE

The prospects for disarmament or for formal restrictions on war have become increasingly complicated by the development of irregular warfare in different forms throughout the world; guerrilla fighting, "subversion," and "resistance."

Guerrilla warfare has become a much greater feature in the conflicts of this century than ever before, and only in this century did it come to receive more than slight attention in Western military theory, although armed action by irregular forces often occurred in earlier times. Clausewitz in his monumental work *On War* devoted one short chapter to the matter, and that came near the end of the thirty chapters of his Book VI, which dealt with the various aspects of "defence." Treating the subject of "arming the people" as a defensive measure against an invader, he formulated the basic conditions of success, and the limitations, but did not discuss the political problems involved. Nor did he make more than slight reference to the Spanish popular resistance to Napoleon's armies, which was the most striking example of guerrilla action in the wars of his time and brought the term into military usage.

A wider and more profound treatment of the subject came, a century later, in T. E. Lawrence's *Seven Pillars of Wisdom*. His masterly formulation of the theory of guerrilla warfare focused on its offensive value and was the product of his combined experience and reflection during the Arab Revolt against the Turks, both as a struggle for independence and as part of the Allied campaign against Turkey. That outlying campaign in the

Middle East was the only one in World War I where guerrilla action exerted an important influence. In the European theatres of war it played no significant part.

In World War II, however, guerrilla warfare became so widespread as to be an almost universal feature. It developed in all the European countries that were occupied by the Germans and most of the Far Eastern countries occupied by the Japanese. Its growth can be traced largely to the deep impression that Lawrence had made, especially on Churchill's mind. After the Germans had overrun France in 1940 and left Britain isolated, it became part of Churchill's war policy to utilise guerrilla warfare as a counter-weapon. The success of such Resistance movements varied. The most effective was in Yugoslavia by the Communist Partisans under Tito's leadership.

Meanwhile, however, a more extensive and prolonged guerrilla war had been waged in the Far East since the 1920s by the Chinese Communists, in whose leadership Mao Tse-tung played an increasingly dominant part.

Since then the combination of guerrilla and subversive war has been pursued with spreading success in neighbouring areas of Southeast Asia and also in other parts of the world, in Africa, starting with Algeria; in Cyprus; on the other side of the Atlantic in Cuba; and now, once again, in the Middle East. Campaigns of this kind are the more likely to continue because it is the only kind of war that fits the conditions of the modern age, while being at the same time well suited to take advantage of social discomfort, racial ferment and nationalistic fervour.

Two of the most significant and influential modern treatises on the subject are Mao Tse-tung's farseeing epistle Yu Chi Chan, produced in 1937, when the Japanese advance into China developed, and Che Guevara's 1960 manual, a textbook synthesis of the methods applied and experience gained in the Cuban Revolution led by Fidel Castro.

As to the role of "resistance," the armed Resistance forces undoubtedly imposed a considerable strain on the Germans during World War II. But when these back-area campaigns are analysed, it would seem that their effect was largely in proportion to the extent to which they were combined with the operations of a strong regular army that was engaging the enemy's front and drawing off his reserves. They rarely became more than a nuisance unless they coincided with the fact, or imminent threat, of a powerful offensive that absorbed the enemy's main attention.

At other times they were less effective than widespread passive resistance and brought far more harm to the people of their own country. They provoked reprisals much severer than the injury inflicted on the enemy. They afforded his troops the opportunity for violent action that is always a relief to the nerves of a garrison in an unfriendly country. The material damage that the guerrillas produced directly, and indirectly in the course of reprisals, caused much suffering among their own people and ultimately became a handicap on recovery after liberation. But the heaviest handicap of all, and the most lasting one, was of a moral kind.

The habit of violence takes much deeper root in irregular warfare than it does in regular warfare. In the latter it is counteracted by the habit of obedience to constituted authority, whereas the former makes a virtue of defying authority and violating rules. It becomes very difficult to rebuild a country, and a stable state, on such an undermined foundation.

A realisation of the dangerous aftermath of guerrilla warfare came to me in reflection on Lawrence's campaigns in Arabia and our discussions on the subject. My book on those campaigns, and exposition of the theory of guerrilla warfare, was taken as a guide by numerous leaders of commando units and resistance movements in the last war. But I was beginning to have doubts, not of its immediate efficacy but of its long-term effects. It seemed that they could be traced, like a thread running through the persisting troubles that we, as the Turks' successors, were suffering in the same area where Lawrence had spread the Arab Revolt.

These doubts were deepened when re-examining the military history of the Peninsula War, a century earlier, and reflecting on the subsequent history of Spain. In that war, Napoleon's defeat of the Spanish regular armies was counterbalanced by the success of the guerrilla bands that replaced them. As a popular uprising against a foreign conqueror, it was one of the most effective on record. It did more than Wellington's victories to loosen Napoleon's grip on Spain and undermine his power. But it did not bring peace to liberated Spain. For it was followed by an epidemic of armed revolutions that continued in quick succession for half a century and broke out again in this century.

It is not too late to learn from the experience of history. However tempting the idea may seem of replying to our opponents' "camouflaged war" activities by counteroffensive moves of the same kind, it would be wiser to devise and pursue a counter-strategy of a more subtle and farseeing kind.

THE PROBLEM OF WORLD ORDER

For the prevention of war, the obvious solution is a world federation, to which all the nations would agree to surrender their absolute sovereignty; their present claim to be final judge of their own policy in all respects and in any disagreement which affects their interest.

Regrettable as it may seem to the idealist, the experience of history provides little warrant for the belief that real progress, and the freedom that makes progress possible, lies in unification. For where unification has been able to establish unity of ideas it has usually ended in uniformity, paralysing the growth of new ideas. And where the unification has merely brought about an artificial or imposed unity, its irksomeness has led through discord to disruption.

Vitality springs from diversity, which makes for real progress so long as there is mutual toleration, based on the recognition that worse may come from an attempt to suppress differences than from acceptance of them. For this reason the kind of peace that makes progress possible is best assured by mutual checks created by a balance of forces; alike in the sphere of internal politics and of international relations. In the international sphere, the "balance of power" was a sound theory so long as the balance was preserved. But the frequency with which the "balance of power" or, as now described, "the balance of terror" has become unbalanced, thereby precipitating war, has produced a growing urge to find a more stable solution, either by fusion or federation.

Federation is the more hopeful method, since it embodies the life-giving principle of cooperation, whereas unification represents the principle of monopoly. And any monopoly of power leads to ever-repeated demonstration of the historical truth epitomised in Lord Acton's famous dictum "All power corrupts, and absolute power corrupts absolutely." From that danger even a federation is not immune, so that the greatest care should be taken to ensure the mutual checks and balancing factors necessary to correct the natural effect of constitutional unity.

Federation has proved effective in preserving peace among different nationalities in successively large groupings. Where it has been adopted it has stood the test of crises. Although the United States of America is the most commonly quoted evidence of its success, the Swiss Confederation is in some ways a more remarkable case. It is painfully clear, however, that the idea of world federation has no practical chance of acceptance in the near future.

THE PROBLEM OF WORLD FAITH

As a historian of our own times, I have had only too much chance to observe how legends spring up around living figures and how the acts and words of any leader or prophet become encrusted with stories that have no foundation in fact. The greater the personal devotion they inspire, the deeper the crust becomes. If this process takes place under modern conditions, where there are so many fact-finding checks, how much more likely that it occurred in a period where an historical sense had hardly developed and checks were lacking.

As a student of ancient history, moreover, I was only too well aware that the idea of a scrupulous fidelity to facts was uncommon even in the writers of history in the ancient world. Most of them were concerned mainly to bring out a new lesson. While scrupulousness about historical facts would have been a new idea to them it would have seemed almost irrelevant to religious teachers. The gospels were compiled as a basis for religious instruction and worship, not for the service of history. That is an essential difference of purpose which cannot be overlooked.

The oldest gospel manuscripts belong to the fourth century A.D. They are copies of copies so that there was an immensely long interval during which copyists might alter the original text to fit the religious ideas of their own generation. Biblical scholars have to base themselves on nothing more definite than tradition in ascribing the origin of the earliest written gospels to the second half of the first century A.D. If they are correct in their deduction, which is really speculation, there is still no means of telling how much they were altered by editing in the course of three hundred years; a period that abounded in controversy and schisms in the Church.

Even on the most hopeful estimate there was still an interval of a generation during which the disciples' memories were in oral circulation; more than long enough for any memory to be coloured and altered by emotional retrospect, as well as by subsequent circumstances. For we have to remember that the disciples were preaching their faith in face of doubt and opposition. They were an exception to all experience if they did not tend to "improve" their Master's sayings and acts in order to meet criticism and carry conviction.

At the same time Christian doctrine was itself in evolution, with consequent effect on its textbooks. I can understand, but consider extremely unreasonable, that thinking men should continue to believe in the same myths and dogmatic conventions that developed in the extremely superstitious mental atmosphere of the Levantine-Roman world two thousand years ago, in a creed that was defined as a result of the most appalling political "wirepulling" and imposed by the despotic power of a couple of credulous and superstitious Roman emperors, who were mainly concerned with acquiring the best "magic" to help their ambitions for power.

I have found in dealing with men of fine character that if they are devout and orthodox Christians one cannot depend on their word as well as if they are not. The good man who is a good churchman is apt to subordinate truth to what he thinks will prove good. That is not surprising, for anyone who had a keen taste for truth would find it difficult to swallow as historical fact much that he does without difficulty. His fervent belief seems to make him insensitive to the point of being credulous.

Many Christian scholars will admit in one breath of the impossibility of bringing to light the historical Jesus, yet speak in their next breath of the incidents in the Gospel narrative just as if they were factually true. That capacity shows insensitivity to the flavour of different shades of truth.

The Church has created, and continues to create, needless and endless difficulties for itself by the excessive emphasis that it has given to the historical aspect of Christianity. If it were only willing to present the Christian story as spiritual truth, these difficulties could be overcome while its progress would be all the better assured. For it could thus do more to bring out the sense of continuous revelation and evolution, teaching mankind to look forward rather than backward, as it has done to a perhaps excessive extent.

The *Old Testament* is interesting and valuable when treated as a study of the evolution of religious ideas. As an exposition of religion, for incorporation in our services, much of it is barbarous and debasing. Even the *New Testament's* presentation of God often falls below good standards.

The sands of history form an uncertain foundation on which to establish a creed composed of factual statements. We can rest broad conclusions on these sands, but if we pin our faith to details they are liable to be washed away by the incoming sea of knowledge, and faith may crumble. If we rest on the broad truth of experience, we become more conscious of, and better able to breathe in, the spirit that moves above the ground level of consciousness. That is the breath of life.

I will state very simply how I came to find evidence of God that was convincing to reason. It was that an unworldly current of goodness has been maintained, and proved insuppressible, in a world where evil flourishes and selfishness has obvious advantages. By human standards there is no sense in self-sacrifice and helping others at one's own expense. Yet that unselfish motive has been manifested in innumerable cases. Can it be explained save by the presence of a higher source of inspiration?

The best of men have been conscious of being no more than windows through which comes a light that is not of their own making but like spiritual sunshine. Or to put it another way, they are merely receiving sets tuned in to the wave length of a spiritual "radio" transmission. They can dust their window panes. They can improve their receptivity. But they are aware that the Source is outside, far beyond their ken.

All this is only a modern way of expressing the "truth beyond human understanding" which the compilers of the gospels tried to convey by describing the incoming of the Holy Spirit in terms of his descent in the shape of a dove. Man's "pictures" of God vary; His inspiration is constant. Ideas of God, and forms of belief, naturally differ and change. For these develop in our minds, and our limited human minds are not capable of understanding His boundless mind. But we can feel God with less difficulty, because we do not formulate anything, as we are bound to do in thinking. His spirit can thus touch ours in a more direct way, and we get a purer breath of it.

I believe we were given minds to think, to search for the truth behind conventions and myths. I like to think that the gift came from a personal God, in the deepest sense of the term, and think that the investment of this creative force with a higher form of personality is more reasonable than to regard it as purely blind materialism.

We are given minds to use, and there can be no better use for them than religious thinking. But we should humbly recognize there may be different paths and feel in sympathy with all other travellers. The difficulties that arise in religious doctrine and history too often drive thoughtful people into a state of no belief. But for my own part I have found that the difficulties tend to disappear if one remembers that such doctrine and history was compiled by human interpreters, humanly liable to mistakes.

Once that is realized it does not matter if science and history show that many of their statements are not factually true. The vital quality is the spiritual truth, not the material facts. Doubts of these become unimportant if one regards the *Bible* not as historical record in the ordinary human sense but as divine parable on the grand scale. The Church feared that faith could not survive the shock if the book of Genesis was shown to be factually incorrect. By its reluctance to admit the possibility, it did more to shake faith in itself than in religion. Looking back now, its fears seem as excessive as its arguments seem ludicrous. Yet it now shows the same fear of admitting that much of the *New Testament* may be non-historical.

If we profess to believe in the Holy Spirit, we should have sufficient faith to rely on that guidance in the evolution of religious ideas. The further I have gone in study and thought the more I have become impressed by the convergence, as distinct from the coincidence, of all the great religious and philosophical thinkers on their uppermost levels. To put it another way, it seems to me that the spiritual development of humanity as a whole is like a pyramid, or a mountain peak, where all angles of ascent tend to converge the higher they climb.

On the one hand this convergent tendency, and the remarkable degree of agreement that is to be found on the higher levels, appears to me the strongest argument from experience that morality is absolute and not merely relative and that religious faith is not a delusion. On the other hand, it seems to me the most encouraging assurance of further progress, if only those who pursue spiritual truth can be brought to recognize their essential community of spirit and learn to make the most of the points where they agree, instead of persistently stressing their differences and emphasising their exclusiveness.

The difficulty of achieving such a spiritual commonwealth is obvious, while the danger to civilization is imminent. Time looks perilously short. It may thus seem unrealistic to pin any hopes of averting world disaster to a revival of religion, even of this wider scope. We have to remember, too, that religion has been an intense spiritual force only for the few. For the many, it has been mainly influential as a mould of thought and behaviour. Yet from this very reflection comes the gleam of a reasonable hope. A partial change in thought and behaviour would mean less than a spiritual transformation, but it might suffice to gain a breathing space for the peoples to recover their balance and for religion to gain a deeper hold.

History justifies such moderate hopes. Twice already our civilization in the West has been rescued by the revival of a code that was based on moral values. The cult of chivalry did quite as much as the efforts of the Church to bring Europe out of the Dark Ages. The second time was after the catastrophic wars of the seventeenth century which were nourished by the violence of religious passions, following the split in the Church. A sense of the fatal consequences grew and produced a habit of restraint.

The same truth has been realized, and more systematically applied on the other side of the world from the sixth century B.C., when Confucius and his followers helped to save Chinese civilization and give it a new lease on life unparalleled in length by teaching a gospel of good manners. We in the West might learn much from the Confucian wisdom in emphasising, and cultivating, good habits as well as good hearts. Confucianism perceived the close and reciprocal relationship of good manners and good morals.

Manners are apt to be regarded as a surface polish. That is a superficial view. They arise from an inward control. A fresh realisation of their importance is needed in the world today, and their revival might prove the salvation of civilization. For only manners in the deeper sense, of mutual restraint for mutual security, can control the risk that outbursts of temper over political and social issues may lead to mutual destruction in the atomic age.

In its emphasis on the need for a "change of heart," Christianity has been apt to underrate the value of a change of habit. With hearts, a temporary change is easier than with habits, but a profound and permanent change is far more difficult. In demanding so complete a change, Christianity has called for more than the mass of its adherents were capable of achieving, as the record shows.

An emotional impulse has too often passed muster as a spiritual transformation. So long as faith was maintained, the Church has been content with too little in the way of "works." The possible has been neglected in favour of the ideal.

Confucianism was humanly wiser. It recognized, and applied, better than Christianity the truth of experience that was epitomised in Aristotle's observation that "Men acquire a particular quality by constantly acting in a particular way." At the same time the Chinese themselves seem to have found that Confucianism "was not enough." Hence the appeal of Buddhism and Taoism there, often in combination with Confucianism. They provided a more spiritual element that mankind wanted.

The West has tended to emphasise the virtue of the positive, "whatsoever ye would that men should do to you, do ye even so to them."[1] The East has emphasised the virtue of the negative , "do not unto others what you would not they should do unto you." Both the positive and the negative are essential. The world needs a better balance in applying the "Golden Rule" which all religions have in common. All faiths can make their contribution to the working out of God's purpose.

---

1 Paraphrased from the Greek.

CONCLUSIONS

How strange appears today the state of optimism about human progress which prevailed in the last century. It reached its zenith when London's Great Exhibition of 1851 opened in the Crystal Palace and was hailed as the inauguration of a Golden Age, of ever-widening peaceful prosperity assured by scientific and technical progress. That dream has changed into a nightmare. Yet it was not without justification, since all the material conditions for its fulfilment have been developed to an extent surpassing expectation, although the new generations endowed with such potentialities have been led to divert them largely into channels of destruction. The causes and the consequences might both be summed up in the old saying "People who live in glass houses should not throw stones."

Can people learn that lesson before their prospects of prosperity are splintered beyond repair in an orgy of mutual devastation? The best chance may lie in developing a deeper understanding of modern warfare on their part, together with a realisation of their mutual responsibility for the way it has got out of control. The development of means has outstripped the growth of minds.

Science and technology have produced a greater transformation of the physical conditions and apparatus of life in the past hundred years than had taken place in the previous two thousand years. Yet when men turn these tremendous new powers to a war purpose, they employ them as recklessly as their ancestors employed the primitive means of the past, and they pursue the same traditional ends without regard to the difference of effect.

Indeed, the Governments of modern nations at war have largely ceased to think of the postwar effects which earlier statesmen were wise enough to bear in mind; a consideration which led in the eighteenth century to a self-imposed limitation of methods. Modern nations have reverted to a more primitive extreme, akin to the practices of warfare between barbaric hordes that were armed with spear and sword, at the same time as they have become possessed of science-given instruments for multiple destruction at long range.

The germs of war find a focus in the convenient belief that "the end justifies the means." Each new generation repeats this argument while succeeding generations have had reason to say that the end their predecessors thus pursued was never justified by the fulfilment conceived. If there is one lesson that should be clear from history it is that bad means deform the end, or deflect its course thither. I would suggest the corollary that, if we take care of the means, the end will take care of itself.

A fervent faith in one particular means may be justified by its actual value in relation to other means, yet err by obscuring the higher value of its disappearance as a contribution to the end. To give an example, those British soldiers who after World War I argued that the tank was the prime factor have been proved right by the experience of World War II, and especially those who visualised it as prime in a combination rather than as an absolute sovereign. At the same time they should also have been able to see that a peace-desiring country had more to gain on balance by a general abolition of tanks. For any frustration of offensive potentialities favours the defence, which in turn promotes the prospects of peace.

Truth is a spiral staircase. What looks true on one level may not be true on the next higher level. A complete vision must extend vertically as well as horizontally; not only seeing the parts in relation to one another but embracing the different planes.

Ascending the spiral, it can be seen that individual security increases with the growth of society, that local security increases when linked to a wider organization, that national security increases when nationalism decreases and would become much greater if each nation's claim to sovereignty were merged in a super-national body. Every step that science achieves in reducing space and time emphasizes the necessity of political integration and a common morality. The advent of the atomic era makes that development more vitally urgent. A movement of the spirit as well as of the mind is needed to attain it.

Only second to the futility of pursuing ends reckless of the means is that of attempting progress by compulsion. History shows how often it leads to reaction. It also shows that the surer way is to generate and diffuse the idea of progress, providing a light to guide men, not a whip to drive them. Influence on thought has been the most influential factor in history, though, being less obvious than the effects of action, it has received less attention, even from writers of history. There is a general recognition that man's capacity for thought has been responsible for all human progress, but not yet an adequate appreciation of the historical effect of contributions to thought in comparison with that of spectacular action. Seen with a sense of proportion, the smallest permanent enlargement of men's thought is a greater achievement, and ambition, than the construction of something material that crumbles, the conquest of a kingdom that collapses, or the leadership of a movement that ends in a rebound.

In the conquest of mind-space it is the inches, consolidated, that count. Also for the spread and endurance of an idea the originator is dependent on the self-development of the receivers and transmitters; far more dependent than is the initiator of an action upon its executants. In the physical sphere subordination can serve as a substitute for cooperation and, although inferior, can go a long way toward producing effective action. But the progress of ideas, if it is to be a true progress, depends on cooperation in a much higher degree and on a higher kind of cooperation.

In this sphere the leader may still be essential, but instead of fusing individuals into a mass through the suppression of their individuality and the contradiction of their thought, the lead that he gives only has effect, lighting effect, in proportion to the elevation of individuality and the expansion of thought. For collective action it suffices if the mass can be managed; collective growth is only possible through the freedom and enlargement of individual minds. It is not the man, still less the mass, that counts, but the many.

Once the collective importance of each individual in helping or hindering progress is appreciated, the experience contained in history is seen to have a personal, not merely a political, significance. What can the individual learn from history as a guide to living? Not what to do but what to strive for. And what to avoid in striving. The importance and intrinsic value of behaving decently. The importance of seeing clearly; not least of seeing himself clearly.

To face life with clear eyes, desirous to see the truth, and to come through it with clean hands, behaving with consideration for others, while achieving such conditions as enable a man to get the best out of life, is enough for ambition: and a high ambition. Only as a man progresses toward it does he realize what effort it entails and how large is the distance to go.

It is strange how people assume that no training is needed in the pursuit of truth. It is stranger still that this assumption is often manifest in the very man who talks of the difficulty of determining what is true. We should recognize that for this pursuit anyone requires at least as much care and training as a boxer for a fight or a runner for a marathon. He has to learn how to detach his thinking from every desire and interest, from every sympathy and antipathy; like ridding oneself of superfluous tissue, the "tissue" of untruth which all human beings tend to accumulate for their own comfort and protection. And he must keep fit, to become fitter. In other words, he must be true to the light he has seen.

He may realize that the world is a jungle. But if he has seen that it could be better for anyone if the simple principles of decency and kindliness were generally applied, then he must in honesty try to practice these consistently and to live, personally, as if they were general. In other words, he must follow the light he has seen.

Since he will be following it through a jungle, however, he should bear in mind the supremely practical guidance provided nearly two thousand years ago: "Behold, I send you forth as sheep in the midst of wolves: be ye therefore wise as serpents, and harmless as doves."